*International Crises
and the Role of Law*

THE CUBAN
MISSILE CRISIS

ABRAM CHAYES

THE CUBAN
MISSILE CRISIS

*International Crises
and the Role of Law*

Published under the auspices
of the American Society of International Law

1974

OXFORD UNIVERSITY PRESS

New York and London

© Oxford University Press 1974
Library of Congress Catalogue Card Number: 74-75041
Printed in the United States of America

For A.H.C.

FOREWORD

IF we want law and legal institutions to play larger and more effective roles in coping with international conflict, we shall need to understand more clearly the roles they now play. This book is one significant step in the search for such understanding. It is the product of a keen and experienced mind looking closely at one international crisis to learn more about the ways in which law affected—and failed to affect—decisions that were being made.

Under the auspices of the American Society of International Law, a group of us set out, individually and collectively, to learn more about the roles which law plays in the making of decisions at a time of crisis—a crisis which involves issues of war and peace. That legal considerations do play various roles in many important government decisions is clear. It is also clear that many other factors—military, political, economic, psychological, historical, cultural, social, and so forth—also have effect on such decisions. Little is to be gained through argument over the comparative importance in any one decision of the different contributing elements. That law played a ten per cent role or a sixty per cent role tells us nothing about how to increase that role. What one needs to know is not *how much* did law affect a given decision, but *how*. What are the different ways in which law and legal institutions affect what happens in international affairs? This book is part of the quest for useful categories of thought to help us all to understand better how international law works and how it fails to work. It is part of the search for practical insights that may lay a foundation for measures designed to expand or strengthen the roles which law plays.

Work of the American Society of International Law in this sphere was made possible by a generous grant of the Old Dominion Foundation (a predecessor to the Andrew W. Mellon Foundation). This monograph has been commissioned and is published under the auspices of the American Society of International Law. Although the author retains full responsibility for the text, an earlier draft of the text was reviewed and discussed by a panel of members of the Society in furtherance of the project. As chairman of the panel, I would like to express our appreciation to the Foundation, to the Society, and particularly to its Executive Director, Professor Stephen M. Schwebel, for supporting and guiding this project from conception to fruition.

ROGER FISHER

Harvard Law School

PREFACE

WORK on this book was begun in 1965–6, in England, under a grant from the Carnegie Corporation. It was an opportunity to set down my reactions soon after I left the State Department when the events were fresh in my mind, and I am most grateful to the Carnegie Corporation for providing it.

Because the missile crisis so dramatically illuminates the interrelations of law and foreign policy decision, it has been a recurrent focus of my work since then. In these bouts, I have often had the company of Dean Thomas Ehrlich of the Stanford Law School and Professor Andreas F. Lowenfeld of the New York University Law School, comrades in the action itself and later in academic reflection. Our joint work on the Cuban missile problem for a collection of teaching materials, *International Legal Process*, was invaluable to me; and Professor Lowenfeld, especially, has been painstaking in his comments and criticisms on the present manuscript.

Lectures almost every year at the Naval War College have given me the chance to pull my current thinking together periodically. And I am grateful to the American Society of International Law, its Executive Director Stephen Schwebel and Director of Studies John Lawrence Hargrove—both of whom shared some of the action in 1962—and to my colleague, Professor Roger Fisher, who organized the sponsoring ASIL Panel, providing not only the occasion for completing the work, but valuable support and criticism.

Anyone writing on the Cuban missiles must acknowledge an obligation to Elie Abel, whose book *The Missile Crisis*, written shortly after the events and based on painstaking personal interviews, remains by far the best detailed account. A brilliant recent work, *Essence of Decision* by Graham Allison has thrown floods of new light on much-travelled terrain. The numerous citations and shorter quotations of these works are evidence of their importance to me, and my thanks are due for permission to print several longer passages.

Government lawyers, present and past, have added greatly to the value of the study. Among them, Ambassador Leonard

C. Meeker, my Deputy in the Office of Legal Adviser, provided factual detail and substantive comment. Norbert Schlei, formerly Assistant Attorney General, Office of Legal Counsel, called my attention to the existence of the Justice Department memorandum printed in Appendix I, and supplied his own recollections of the events. Benjamin Foreman, Assistant General Counsel for International Security Affairs, Department of Defense, made available the excerpt from the Defense Department legal opinion.

Like all professors, I am indebted to all my students, not only those who worked on this particular book. Confronting classes throughout the late sixties and early seventies did not leave a participant much room for complacency, and my conclusions have measurably changed in response. Two students deserve special recognition: Ms. Toni Pickard, now a Professor of Law at King's College, Hamilton, Ontario, probed and prodded the earliest drafts to their very great benefit; and Lewis Paper, at a later stage, helped with notes and documentation.

A series of secretaries shared the chores of typing and proofing: Mary Beth McGrail, Linda Carter, and Jane Coakley.

Finally, a special problem is raised by the treatment of the Executive Committee meeting of 19 October 1962, details of which bulk large in my analysis and account for much of what is new in it. A memorandum of that meeting was prepared at my request by Mr. Meeker, who as Deputy Legal Adviser attended in my absence. Copies of the memorandum were retained in his files and my own. The document was not further circulated and was not classified. I had hoped to publish the text of the memorandum in this book and received Mr. Meeker's personal permission to do so, subject to State Department approval. The Department not only withheld its approval, but sought to classify the document retroactively. In these days, after the Pentagon Papers and other massive leaks, it would have been only minimally courageous to have published the memorandum, nothwithstanding. But Mr. Meeker is still an officer in the Department, and a valuable one. And I was sensitive to the risk that publication might affect him adversely. So I have resorted to extensive and close paraphrase of the text. In a subsequent edition, if there is one, the inhibiting considerations will have disappeared and the memorandum will be published in full. Meanwhile, footnote 34, at p. 15, stands as another small monument to follies committed in the name of secrecy.

CONTENTS

I

PRELIMINARIES

i

Inter arma silent leges. Without too much difficulty, the maxim can be extended to cover situations where the vital interests of the state are threatened. The Cuban missile crisis was such a case. Or so, at least, it was perceived by the President and most of the men upon whom he relied in deciding upon his course of action.

It is the harshest test of international law, perhaps an unfair test, to ask whether and how it affected the decisions and acts of men who saw themselves as grappling with issues of national survival. Dean Acheson, a distinguished lawyer and diplomat, was content to say 'The power, position and prestige of the United States had been challenged by another state; and law simply does not deal with such questions of ultimate power— power that comes close to the sources of sovereignty.'[1]

It is tempting to let the matter rest there. The outcome of the Cuban missile crisis can be reckoned a success for the United States by almost any standard. The Soviet missiles were removed. There was no war. A decade after the event, it is seen as a watershed marking the end of the harshest phase of the Cold War, after which the two contestants moderated their voices and their tactics.[2] Harold Macmillan, an *aficionado* of international crisis,

---

[1] Dean Acheson, in [1963] Proc. Am. Soc. Int'l L. 14.

[2] Hilsman, *To Move a Nation* 228–9 (1967) (hereafter cited Hilsman): 'Whether the Cuban missile crisis marks a turning point in world history is as yet impossible to say. The Soviets put missiles into Cuba in an attempt to solve a set of problems. . . . The irony is that these same problems, which brought the world so near to nuclear war, later brought about the so-called *détente*—a relaxation of Cold War tensions. For it was the same pressures that led the Soviets to put missiles in Cuba that later led them to take up Kennedy's proposal for a treaty banning nuclear testing. . . .

'The threat of nuclear war was not eliminated from the world by the events of October 1962, nor was there a reconciliation between East and West. But if either of these two objectives ever is attained, historians may well mark the Cuban missile crisis of 1962 as the beginning.'

Sorensen, *Kennedy* 719 (1965) (hereafter cited Sorensen): 'The Cuban missile crisis, Harold Macmillan told the House of Commons shortly after it

called it 'masterly'.[3] Denis Healey, no gentle critic, said it 'could be cited as a model in any textbook on diplomacy'.[4] What does it matter, then, whether the operation was conducted by the book legally as well?

It is not so easy for international law scholarship to ignore the legal aspects of the crisis, however.[5] To begin with, there is a problem of characterization: were the vital interests of the United States really engaged? Latter-day criticism has argued that they were not.[6] If the missile emplacement had been successfully completed, the number of Soviet missiles capable of reaching the

---

ended, represented "one of the great turning points in history". The autumn of 1962, said President Kennedy, if not a turning point, was at least "a climactic period . . . even though its effects can't be fully perceived now. . . . Future historians looking back at 1962 may well mark this year as the time when the tide . . . began [to turn]."

'Time will tell whether subsequent events—in Peking, Moscow, Dallas and elsewhere—have altered or will yet alter the accuracy of those prophecies. But in 1962–1963 little time elapsed before the impact of that crisis was affecting Soviet–American relations. . . .'

Cf. Allison, *Essence of Decision: Explaining the Cuban Missile Crisis* 39 (1971) (hereafter cited Allison).

[3] Kennedy, *Thirteen Days* 17 (1969) (hereafter cited Kennedy) (Introduction by Harold Macmillan).

[4] George, *The Limits of Coercive Diplomacy* 132 (1971).

[5] For other legal analyses of the Cuban missile crisis, see Campbell, 'The Cuban Crisis and the UN Charter: An Analysis of the United States Position', 16 Stan. L. Rev. 160 (1963); Wright, 'The Cuban Quarantine', 57 Am. J. Int'l L. 546 (1963); Alford, 'The Cuban Quarantine of 1962: An Inquiry into Paradox and Persuasion', 4 Va. J. Int'l L. 35 (1964); Partan, 'The Cuban Quarantine: Some Implications for Self-Defense', [1963] Duke L. J. 696; Meeker, 'Defensive Quarantine and the Law', 57 Am. J. Int'l L. 515 (1963); Raymond, Legal Implications of the Cuban Crisis', 3 Santa Clara L. 126 (1963); Christol and Davis, 'Maritime Quarantine: The Naval Interdiction of Offensive Weapons and Associated Material to Cuba', 57 Am. J. Int'l L. 525 (1963); panel discussion: 'The Cuba Quarantine: Implications for the Future', [1963] Proc. Am. Soc. Int'l L. 1; Fenwick, 'Quarantine Against Cuba: Legal or Illegal', 57 Am. J. Int'l L. 588 (1963); Re, 'The Quarantine of Cuba in International Law', 6 JAG Bull. 3 (1964); McDevitt, 'The UN Charter and the Cuba Quarantine', 17 JAG J. 71 (1963); Valentine, 'U.S. Naval Quarantine of Cuba: New Wine in a New Bottle', 23 Fed. B. J. 244 (1963); Standard, 'The United States Quarantine of Cuba and the Rule of Law', 49 ABA J. 744 (1963); II Chayes, Ehrlich, and Lowenfeld, *International Legal Process* 1057–149 (1968).

[6] E.g., Steel, *'Endgame'*, *N.Y. Review of Books*, 13 March, 1969, p.15, col. 1; FitzSimmons, *The Kennedy Doctrine* 126–72 (1969); Walton, *Cold War and Counterrevolution: The Foreign Policy of John F. Kennedy* 103–42 (1972).

United States would have been doubled.[7] That would have made a certain difference in the respective military positions of the parties. In particular, the United States strategic bomber force would have been more vulnerable, at least for a time. These missiles, approaching from the south, could not be detected by the warning net, facing north-east, that gave the bombers time to get off the ground in case of attack.[8]

Nevertheless, the United States would have retained at least a two-to-one superiority in missiles over the U.S.S.R. The second-strike capability, upon which deterrence of Soviet nuclear attack is thought to depend, would not have been threatened. For Secretary McNamara, 'seven-to-one missile "superiority", one-to-one missile "equality", one-to-seven "inferiority"—the three postures were nearly identical'.[9] In the first meetings on the crisis he argued 'A missile is a missile. It makes no great difference whether you are killed by a missile from the Soviet Union or from Cuba.'[10] This analysis led him to urge, at first, the mildest of responses: a deflating announcement or a diplomatic approach.[11]

On the question of whether the missiles would have changed the strategic balance, President Kennedy said in his summary of the events some weeks later: 'It would have appeared to, and appearances contribute to reality.'[12] And there is widespread agreement that, if the Soviets had succeeded in their effort, it would have been a major political reverse for the United States. Many have doubted that the appearances and political costs were worth a risk of nuclear war that the President himself estimated at between 33 and 50 per cent.[13] Certainly it is difficult for the international lawyer to accept the conclusion that they add up to a 'vital interest' sufficient to warrant the claim of an absolute exemption from constraints and methods prescribed by law.

Among writers on international law, it is widely, perhaps generally held that, from a legal point of view, the question

---

[7] Allison at 44, 54; cf. Hilsman at 201.
[8] Allison at 54; Abel, *The Missile Crisis* 52 (1966) (hereafter cited Abel).
[9] Allison at 195.
[10] Abel at 51.
[11] Id. at 52–3; Hilsman at 195; Allison at 195–6.
[12] [1962] *Public Papers of the Presidents, John F. Kennedy* 898.
[13] Allison at 1; but see id. at 218, where Allison observes that '. . . it is difficult to believe that the President actually felt that the chance of war was one-in-three, . . .'

whether or not the strategic balance was changed was simply beside the point. Since 1945, when the U.N. Charter proscribed the threat or use of force, a state is no longer legally free to use force unilaterally to protect its interests, however vital, unless 'an armed attack occurs'.[14] This view of the law may be right or wrong; and the law may be wise or foolish in seeking thus to regulate the decisions of states. But, for one devoted to international law, it is not enough to dismiss these issues by saying simply that 'law does not deal with questions of ultimate power'.

The series of studies of which this is one addresses the question 'how' law enters the policy-making process, not 'how much'. The formulation is perhaps disingenuous. We are not asking for a catalogue of the ways in which law *might* have affected the course of action chosen. We are asking about the ways in which it *did* influence action. To be included in the catalogue any particular 'way' must, at least arguably, have been substantial among the relevant elements and considerations that went into the amalgam of decision.

We shall stop at that. We cannot ask for a demonstration that legal considerations dictated decision. Graham Allison, in his recent study of the affair of the missiles in Cuba, brilliantly discredits what may be called the anthropomorphic fallacy in policy analysis—the tendency to think of government decisions as the product of a single, rationally calculating brain.[15] Discussion of the role of law in foreign-policy decision is especially prone to this anthropomorphic fallacy. Both analyst and audience tend to see the law as a rule or norm, typically a prohibition, addressed to a man, or to a monolithic subject of law. The decision-maker is visualized as a client getting advice from his lawyer about whether a proposed course of action is 'legal' or not. The role of law in the decisional process is settled by whether the decision-maker 'followed' this advice—particularly if it was negative.

Even measured on this crude scale, the law does not come off too badly in the missile crisis. The State Department lawyer, as we shall see, advised that the situation in Cuba did not constitute armed attack on any country, warranting a unilateral response, but that the law would support a 'defensive quarantine' of Cuba

---

[14] See Russell, *A History of the United Nations Charter* 669–775 (1958); Franck, 'Who killed Article 2(4)? or: Changing Norms Governing the use of Force by States', 64 Am. J. Int'l L. 809 (1970).

[15] Allison, *Essence of Decision: Explaining the Cuban Missile Crisis* (1971).

if it were authorized by the Organization of American States (O.A.S) under the Rio Treaty.[16] The military advice to the President was for an immediate invasion of Cuba or for a massive air strike, involving some 500 sorties.[17] This course was supported by the most prominent practitioners of *realpolitik* among the President's advisers.[18] It was their views the President rejected, not the lawyers'.

We would not conclude from this that military considerations played no role in the decision-making process. Conversely, I do not base a claim for the role of law on the congruence of the final decision with the lawyers' advice. It is no more possible to demonstrate 'proximate' causation here than in any other human process. The weight and consequence of legal advice in the final decision, like the weight and consequence of military judgment or Kennedy's machismo or the bureaucratic rigidity of the Air Force are, and must remain, unknowable.

ii

The missile crisis has been called the finest hour of the Kennedy administration.[19] Despite the work of revisionists, left[20] and right,[21] accounts of the episode exude an air of 'we happy few,' which this study has, no doubt, failed to suppress completely. There is an almost irresistible temptation for anyone who was connected with the events, no matter now remotely, to 'strip his sleeves and show his scars and say "These wounds I had on Crispin's day" '.

But scholarship, if it is to be more than action recollected—not to say embellished—in tranquillity, must guard against the human propensity to 'remember with advantages the feats we did

---

[16] See pp. 15–16 *infra*.

[17] Allison at 197–8; the figure of 500 sorties appears id. at 60, 123–6.

[18] This group included Dean Acheson, Douglas Dillon, John McCone, Paul Nitze, Maxwell Taylor, and, for a time, McGeorge Bundy. Abel at 79; Allison at 204 comments that this group 'was not composed of the President's natural allies'.

[19] See nn. 2, 3, 4 *supra;* see also Sorensen at 717, 745; Schlesinger, *A Thousand Days* 840 (1965).

[20] See n. 6 *supra*.

[21] See Acheson, 'Dean Acheson's Version of Robert Kennedy's Version of the Cuban Missile Affair', *Esquire*, Feb. 1969, at 76, in which Mr. Acheson contends that the President's success in resolving the crisis was based largely on 'dumb luck'.

that day'. So that the reader may make his own discount, let me state at the outset my connection with the events discussed in this study. In October 1962, I was the Legal Adviser of the Department of State and as such had formal responsibility for all the law work of the Department.[22] However, during most of the week of decision, I was out of the country. The Office was represented by the Deputy Legal Adviser, Leonard C. Meeker, a career lawyer of fifteen years standing in the Department, who was later to become Legal Adviser and then United States Ambassador to Rumania. I was recalled from Paris on Thursday of the week and did not arrive in Washington until Friday evening, 18 October, after the principal decisions had been taken, at least tentatively. Thereafter, along with an increasing number of the members of the Office, I was continuously engaged, particularly in the preparation of the positions before the O.A.S. and the U.N. and the drafting of the quarantine proclamation itself.

I hope to demonstrate that law was one of the critical forces moulding decision. But the Allison book, the fullest and most recent account of the crisis, has no index entry for law. The other principal narrators—Abel, Hilsman, Schlesinger, Sorensen, and Robert F. Kennedy—make scattered references to legal issues and considerations, but for none of them does it emerge as a major theme.

iii

This study does not attempt to cover the operation of law throughout the missile crisis, from first discovery to final settlement. The method of this series is to analyse the decision process in cross-section, at a single point in time, or, to change the metaphor, in a stop-action photograph. For these purposes, I have chosen to focus on three interrelated decisions about the course of action that was followed: (1) the choice of the blockade, or 'quarantine', as against harsher or milder responses, (2) the decision to seek an O.A.S. authorizing resolution; (3) the manner

[22] For those unfamiliar with the governmental hierarchy, the Legal Adviser in the State Department is the chief legal officer of the Department. He is the equivalent to the general counsel of other governmental departments, and, like them is appointed by the President by and with the advice and consent of the Senate. In 1962, the Legal Adviser's office consisted of approximately 60 lawyers, grouped roughly into teams corresponding to the geographical and functional bureaux of the Department.

and method of the approach to the U.N. Analysis has heretofore focused primarily on the first of these decisions, but all three were in fact complementary and integrated. Together they comprised the programme of action laid out by the President in his speech to the nation and the world on the evening of 22 October, 1962, announcing the presence of nuclear missiles in Cuba and the United States response to it.[23]

The paper begins with a brief review of the factual background, the discovery of the missiles and the discussions among officials leading to the three decisions. Much of this is familiar ground, heavily worked by chroniclers and analysts, to whom the reader is referred for more detail.[24] The new matter in this account relates primarily to the legal materials and analysis that were before the President's advisers, and this is developed in considerable detail.

The study then considers in turn the principal ways in which law affected, or might be thought to have affected, the course of action adopted. First, as a constraint on action; second, as the basis of justification or legitimation for action; and third, as providing organizational structures, procedures, and forums.

[23] [1962] *Public Papers of the Presidents, John F. Kennedy* 806.

[24] In addition to the accounts principally relied on here—Abel, Allison, Hilsman, Kennedy, Schlesinger, and Sorensen—see Salinger, *With Kennedy* (1967); Sidey, *John F. Kennedy, President* (1967); Tatu, *Power in the Kremlin* (1969); Bartlett and Weintal, *Facing the Brink: An Intimate Study of Crisis Diplomacy* (1967); 'Cuban Crisis: A Step-by-Step Review', *N.Y. Times*, 3 November 1972 p. 1, col. 6; for legal analyses of the crisis see n. 5 *supra*.

II

THE SETTING: FACTS AND LAW

i

SOVIET arms shipments to Cuba, which had been discontinued in early 1962, were resumed towards the end of July, and proceeded through the summer at an accelerating rate. Thirty-seven Soviet cargo ships put in to Cuban ports in the month of August, of which twenty carried arms shipments.[1] New and suspicious types of Soviet vessels were used for some of these shipments. Unloading was done at night and in great secrecy. From the end of July to mid-October when the quarantine was imposed, more than 100 shiploads of arms were dispatched to Cuba from the U.S.S.R.[2] These included 42 medium-range ballistic missiles (MRBMs); 12 intermediate-range ballistic missile (IRBM) launchers plus associated equipment; 42 Ilyushin IL-28 medium-range jet-bombers; 144 surface-to-air anti-aircraft missile (SAM) launchers with related equipment and 4 missiles per launcher; 42 high performance MIG-21 fighter aircraft; assorted cruise missiles and missile-carrying patrol-boats; and 22,000 Soviet troops for construction, operation, and defence of these weapons.[3]

United States intelligence kept these movements under continuous surveillance by all available means, most effectively by overhead reconnaissance with U-2s flying above 75,000 feet.[4] On the basis of the information derived from all sources, government intelligence agencies were in agreement until the latter part of September that the build-up in Cuba was confined to defensive systems, ringing the island with surface-to-air and coastal defence missiles.[5]

Badly scarred by the Bay of Pigs fiasco, the Kennedy administration was both vulnerable and sensitive on the question of

---

[1] Allison at 103; see also Hilsman at 170.

[2] Id. at 159.

[3] Allison at 104–5.

[4] Id. at 119; Hilsman at 167–8; Abel at 21–3.

[5] Hilsman at 170–3; Allison at 118–21; Abel at 17; Kennedy at 28; Sorensen at 670.

Cuba. Republicans, relying on public opinion polls showing growing public concern about Soviet influence in Cuba, served notice that Cuba would be 'the dominant issue' of the November Congressional campaign.[6] With Senators Keating, Capehart and Goldwater in the van, they excoriated the President's 'do nothing' policy.[7] Capehart called for an invasion of Cuba.[8] Keating, the most persistent and vocal of the attackers, made repeated head-lines with warnings, based on self-proclaimed but unrevealed intelligence, of Soviet missiles in Cuba.[9]

In response the President twice made formal statements in-sisting that the build-up to that point had been defensive in character. On 4 September he said:

There is no evidence of any organized combat force in Cuba from any Soviet bloc country; of a violation of the 1934 treaty relating to Guan-tanamo; of the presence of offensive ground-to-ground missiles; or of other significant offensive capability either in Cuban hands or under Soviet direction and guidance. Were it to be otherwise, the gravest issues would arise.[10]

On 13 September, after a Soviet statement citing threats of a United States attack on Cuba, the President reiterated his con-clusion 'that these new shipments do not constitute a serious threat to any other part of this hemisphere'.[11] He went on to say:

... unilateral military intervention on the part of the United States can-not currently be either required or justified, and it is regrettable that loose talk about such action in this country might serve to give a thin color of legitimacy to the Communist pretenses that such a threat exists.[12]

He emphasized again that the United States would regard it as threatening 'if Cuba should ever . . . become an offensive military base of significant capacity for the Soviet Union'. In that event, he stated, 'this country will do whatever must be done to protect

---

[6] Ibid. See also Kennedy at 25; Abel at 11–13; see Olsen, 'G.O.P. Backs use of Troops in Cuba', *N.Y. Times*, 8 Sept. 1962, p. 2, col. 4.

[7] Sorensen, at 669; Hilsman at 196–7; and Abel at 11–13.

[8] Kennedy at 25; Abel at 12; cf. *N.Y. Times*, 3 Sept. 1962, p. 2, col. 5.

[9] Hilsman at 177–80; Sorensen at 670; Abel at 41. See, e.g., 'Keating Opposes a Deal on Cuba', *N.Y. Times*, 10 Sept. 1962, p. 6, col. 3.

[10] *N.Y. Times*, 5 Sept. 1962, p. 2, col. 5.

[11] [1962] *Public Papers of the Presidents, John F. Kennedy* 674.

[12] Ibid.

its own security and that of its allies'.[13] A reporter asked how he would 'determine that the build-up in Cuba has lost its defensive guise to become offensive'. The President in reply emphasized 'the presence of offensive military missile capacity or development of military bases'.[14]

Administration spokesmen, in a continuing effort to cool Congressional concern over the situation in Cuba, maintained the position in public speeches and in Congressional testimony that the weapons systems being installed in Cuba were 'basically of a defensive capability'.[15] They rejected out of hand the proposals for invasion or air strikes.[16] Both Secretary Rusk and Vice-President Johnson took the position that a blockade was 'an act of war' and so was also ruled out.[17]

Despite these efforts, there was increasing pressure in Congress for a sweeping resolution against the build-up in Cuba. Senator Dirksen and Congressman Halleck, acting as 'the members of the joint Senate-House Republican leadership', proposed the adoption of a resolution modelled on the Formosa Resolution of 1955,[18] which authorized 'the President of the United States to employ our own armed forces as he deemed necessary to protect those Asiatic islands'.[19] The administration concluded it

[13] [1962] *Public Papers of the Presidents, John F. Kennedy* at 674.

[14] Id. at 675.

[15] Testimony of Under Secretary of State George Ball in Hearings before the House Select Comm. on Export Control, 87th Cong., 2nd Sess. 811 (1962).

[16] E. Speigel, 'Bowles Attacks War Talk on Cuba', *N.Y. Times*, 17 Sept. 1962, p. 1, col. 2. See also Allison at 189. Although the President and other members of the administration considered suggestions of invading Cuba as 'irresponsible', the administration did undertake limited military preparations to offset the appeal of such suggestions and to rebut any inference that it was not concerned by the Soviet activity in Cuba. For instance, on 7 September, the President sought, and subsequently received, authorization to call up 150,000 army reservists in the event that military action was required to respond to the Cuban situation. Kenworthy, 'President Seeks Right To Call Up 150,000 Reservists', *N.Y. Times*, 8 Sept. 1962, p. 1, col. 8.

[17] Hearings on the Situation in Cuba before the Sen. Comm. on Foreign Relations and Sen. Comm. on Armed Services, 87th Cong., 2nd Sess. 35 (1962). Abel at 62.

[18] P. L. 84-4 (29 Jan. 1955).

[19] 108 Cong. Rec. 20054 (1962) (remarks of Senator Dirksen); see also 108 Cong. Rec. 20865 (1962) (remarks of Rep. Halleck). As a result of this initiative, four resolutions were introduced by Republicans in the Senate. Two introduced by Senator Prouty merely authorized the President to employ the country's armed forces to '. . . protect the peace and security of the United States and the

could not block a resolution altogether, and settled for trying to moderate the language.[20] When it was finally passed on 3 October, the text rather closely followed the wording of the President's 13 September statement. Instead of expressly 'authorizing' the use of force it resolved only that 'the United States is determined by whatever means may be necessary, including the use of arms, . . . to prevent in Cuba the creation or use of an externally supported military capability endangering the security of the United States'.[21]

In the midst of the rising political tensions, the United States Intelligence Board, the co-ordinating group for all United States intelligence activities, met on 19 September. Although there were some misgivings, the Board unanimously approved an intelligence estimate concluding 'in effect', according to Roger Hilsman, then State Department Director of Intelligence and Research, that the Soviets would not introduce offensive missiles in Cuba.[22]

---

free world'. 108 Cong. Rec. 19158, 19321 (1962). Another resolution offered by Senator Miller reaffirmed the principles of the Monroe Doctrine and directed the President '. . . to take such action as is necessary to prevent any violation thereof'. 108 Cong. Rec. 19321 (1962). The resolution introduced by Senators Bush and Keating was the most explicitly tied to the situation in Cuba. It declared that the domination of Cuba by 'the international Communist movement jeopardized peace in the Western Hemisphere and violated the right of the Cuban people to self-determination', and asserted that the United States, '. . . under the principles of the Monroe Doctrine, the Inter-American Treaty of Reciprocal Assistance, and Article 51 of the Charter of the United Nations, has the right and obligation to take all necessary actions, in cooperation with other Western Hemisphere nations if possible, and unilaterally if necessary, to end such domination and control and to restore the Republic of Cuba to a government of the people, by the people, and for the people'. Ibid.

[20] Sorensen at 672.

[21] P.L. 87–733 (3 Oct. 1962).

[22] According to Hilsman, the estimate's conclusions were based primarily on three factors. First, '. . . the Soviets realized the Americans would be likely to discover the missiles and would probably react strongly—that, in other words, the likelihood of exposure was high and the probable consequences bad'. Second, deployment of offensive missiles in Cuba would be inconsistent with the caution which the Soviet Union had always exercised in nuclear matters. The Soviet Union had not even placed offensive missiles in Eastern Europe, where their installation would be easier to supervise and less provocative internationally. In addition, 'both air and sea communications between Cuba and the Soviet Union were long, hazardous, and peculiarly vulnerable to American interdiction'. Third, Cuba was a self-appointed member of the

Earlier, on 10 September, the Committee on Overhead Reconnaissance, chaired by McGeorge Bundy, Special Assistant to the
President for National Security Affairs, had met with Secretary
Rusk in attendance. The day before, a Nationalist U-2 had been
downed over mainland China.[23] The Soviet surface-to-air missiles
on the western end of Cuba were or would soon be operational.
Fearing the outcry that might come if another U-2 were to be shot
down, the Committee decided to alter the reconnaissance flight-
pattern to avoid going directly over the western end of the
island.[24] The next overflight of this area was not authorized until
9 October, after a review of evidence gathered since the 19
September Intelligence Board meeting aroused increasing suspicion about Soviet activity there. Further delays ensued, and the
mission was not carried out until Sunday 14 October. It was
flown by Maj. Rudolph Anderson, who was later to become the
only casualty of the missile crisis.

Communist bloc and '. . . the regime and Castro himself were unstable, hardly
to be trusted either as the recipients of really dangerous weapons or as the
hosts for weapons that remained under Soviet control'. Nevertheless, the Board
observed that placement of ballistic missiles in Cuba would significantly
increase Soviet capacity to strike at 'America's heartland', and advised that
continued surveillance of the island be maintained. C.I.A. Director John
McCone, then in Europe on a honeymoon, cabled his reservations about the
estimate's conclusions. McCone suggested that the evidence could support an
argument that the missiles in Cuba were of an offensive nature. McCone had
expressed these same reservations to the President in August. According to
Hilsman the C.I.A. estimators responded with further justification for their
conclusion that the missiles being installed in Cuba at that time were defensive
only. McCone apparently was persuaded, or, in any case, '. . . decided against
bringing his doubts to the attention of other members of the Intelligence
Board or to the President, much less to insist on a change in the estimate, even
though it was his legal right'. Hilsman at 172–3; see also Abel at 23–4; Allison
at 190–2.

[23] Abel at 25; Hilsman at 174.

[24] The decision of the Committee on Overhead Reconnaissance (COMOR)
reflected concern that there should be no repetition of the incident during the
Eisenhower Administration when pilot Gary Francis Powers's U-2 was downed
in the Soviet Union and U-2 flights over the Soviet Union were terminated.
This concern led COMOR to adopt Secretary Rusk's suggestion that, instead
of an end-to-end flight which would require the U-2 to remain over Cuba for a
long period of time, the committee should authorize a flight-pattern that
dipped in and out of Cuban air space. In addition, the pilots were instructed
to avoid the western part of the island. It was not until McCone returned on
4 October that pressure was exerted to resume flights over the western part of
the island. Abel at 25–6; Hilsman at 174, 189–90; Allison at 192.

The photographs revealed that a launching site for Soviet MRBMs was being built in the area of San Cristobal, fifty miles south-west of Havana.[25] These weapons are movable missiles carrying nuclear warheads and capable of delivering them at a range of 1,000 nautical miles. Later photographs showed another site under construction at Sagua la Grande, and two sites for intermediate-range missiles, with an effective range of 2,000 miles at Guanajay and Remedios.[26]

Processing of the first photographs took most of Monday 15 October, and high officials at Defense, State, and the White House were informed during the evening. Bundy brought the news to President Kennedy first thing on Tuesday morning. Within a few hours, the President met with the group of close advisers that was later to be denominated the Executive Committee of the National Security Council. Meetings of this Committee continued on an intensive basis, with increasing support from a gradually widening circle of subordinate officials, until Saturday afternoon, when the President made his decision and it was formally approved by the National Security Council.

ii

The Executive Committee consisted of a dozen or so men— Robert Kennedy names fourteen.[27] Four of these were lawyers by training and profession: Robert Kennedy, the Attorney General; Theodore Sorensen, Special Counsel to the President; George Ball, Under Secretary of State; and Roswell Gilpatric, Deputy Secretary of Defense. Two other lawyers participated in the deliberations of the Committee: Dean Acheson, former Secretary of State, in the earlier phases, and Adlai Stevenson, United States Ambassador to the U.N., somewhat later.[28] This extraordinary concentration might be treated as simply another piece of evidence for the not very novel proposition that a law-school education is one of the best routes to the upper reaches of the United States policy-making establishment. Both George Kennan and

[25] Abel at 28–9; Hilsman at 180; Sorensen at 672–3.
[26] Hilsman at 159; see also the map in id. at 160; Allison at 104.
[27] Kennedy at 30.
[28] Although not a member of the bar, Secretary of State Rusk had attended law school and had for a considerable period been in charge of United Nations affairs in the State Department. Dept. State, *The Biographic Register* ix (1964)

Charles Thayer have maintained that because of the high incidence of lawyers in these positions, American foreign policy characteristically overvalues legal considerations and very often tends to view policy issues as questions of law.[29] Be that as it may, making allowances for all the shifts and turns that occurred in the course of intensive and searching debate, these lawyers, Dean Acheson excepted, exerted consistent influence for restraint and limit in the response to the Cuban missiles.[30]

The legal issues were formally presented at some length by lawyers from the State and Justice Departments and debated at a full session of the Executive Committee on the morning of Friday 19 October.[31] At that time, although there appeared to be a growing consensus for blockade-type action, the decision was by no means clear, and in fact the consensus began to come apart at this very Friday session.[32] The Executive Committee's request for a review of the legal situation was stimulated by a remark on Thursday night by Ambassador Llewellyn Thompson, who had just returned from his tour as Ambassador to the Soviet Union to replace Charles E. Bohlen as Special Assistant to the Secretary of State for Soviet Affairs. Thompson said that the Russians had a penchant for legalities and would be impressed by a good legal case. Lawyers at Justice and State were alerted on Thursday, after Thompson's comments,[33] and on Friday morning, after

[29] Kennan, *American Diplomacy: 1900–1950* 95–103 (1951); Thayer, *Diplomat* 251–3 (1959).

[30] See Kennedy at 37–8 for his own position and that of McNamara; Abel at 63–4, for the positions of Ball and Kennedy; Allison at 196–9 and 202–4 canvasses the views of all the participants in detail. See also Acheson, 'Dean Acheson's Version of Robert Kennedy's Version of the Cuban Missile Affair', *Esquire*, Feb. 1969, p. 76. Sorensen notes that the career diplomats also favoured a blockade. Sorensen at 686.

[31] Abel at 72 states that the legal issues were reviewed by Acheson and Ball before the President himself on Thursday, but none of the other accounts corroborate this.

[32] Kennedy 44–6; Hilsman at 204–6; Sorensen at 692; Abel at 86–9; Allison at 206–8. Dean Acheson and the Joint Chiefs of Staff, with some support from McGeorge Bundy, were primarily responsible for driving a wedge in the consensus which had presumably been reached on Thursday night.

[33] For Thompson's remarks, see Abel at 87. Sorensen at 706. For the start of the legal work, see Abel at 82; Sorensen at 691–2. Meeker states that he was asked on Thursday afternoon to prepare '. . . a paper on legal characterization of the situation and on what the U.S. could do about it'. Letter from Leonard Meeker to Abram Chayes, 21 Apr. 1971. On Friday morning before the

the ritual intelligence briefing that opened Executive Committee meetings, they made their presentations.[34]

Secretary Rusk called first on Mr. Meeker, but the Attorney General intervened and asked that his Deputy, Mr. Katzenbach should speak first. Mr. Katzenbach expressed his view that a declaration of war was unnecessary and that United States military action could be justified in international law on the principle of self-defence.

Mr. Meeker followed. He agreed with the judgment that a declaration of war would not improve the United States position. His analysis was based on the premiss that a 'defensive quarantine' of Cuba would amount to a use of force, which had to be considered in relation to the general prohibition against the use of force in Article 2(4) of the U.N. Charter. Meeker pointed out that there were several recognized exceptions to this prohibition. One of these was self-defence in case of armed attack, but Meeker did not think the situation in Cuba constituted an armed attack on any country. A second exception noted was action by the U.N. under Chapter VII of the Charter, but it was obvious that the

---

ExCom meeting Meeker discussed his paper with Ball, Johnson, and Martin. At that meeting, Meeker suggested, for historical and psychological reasons, the use of the term 'defensive quarantine' instead of 'blockade'. Ibid. The label 'quarantine' was thus born here, although others have made claims to its paternity. It harked back to President Roosevelt's call for a 'quarantine of the aggressors' before the Second World War. See Abel at 73. But it had the further advantage of not implying a characterization of the situation as a 'war', the only circumstance in which, according to traditional U.S. doctrine, a blockade could be instituted. See [1903] Foreign Relations of the United States 417–41, 452–79, 601–13, 788–805; Dept. of Navy, Office of Chief of Naval Operations, *Law of Naval Warfare* §§631–2 (1955). Avoidance of the harsher term thus contributed to the effort to communicate restraint as well as firmness, to the Soviets. See Sorensen at 694. On Sunday Secretary Rusk voiced a concern that use of the word might be regarded as a semantic 'gimmick' but after I reviewed the foregoing considerations with him, he withdrew his reservation.

[34] The following account is based on a number of conversations with participants during or shortly after the crisis. I have also drawn heavily on a memorandum prepared by Mr. Meeker at my request a day or two after the meeting from his notes taken at the meeting. The State Department has declined to permit the full text of the memorandum to be published at this time, but in addition to the copy in my possession, Mr. Meeker has deposited a copy in the Kennedy Library where it will presumably become available in due course. The Meeker memorandum is entirely consistent with the published accounts of the 19 October meeting, see, e.g., Abel at 87–8, but is more detailed on the legal issues.

Security Council would be immobilized, and Meeker thought it was problematical whether the United States could obtain a recommendation from the General Assembly.

A third possibility was presented by the provisions for regional arrangements in Chapter VIII of the U.N. Charter. Meeker emphasized the importance of Article 52, providing that regional arrangements could deal with 'such matters relating to the maintenance of peace and security as are appropriate for regional action'. He concluded that, if the O.A.S. acting under the Rio Treaty approved, a case could be made for the use of force. He pointed to the provisions of Articles 6 and 8 of the Treaty, under which, he argued, the organization could take measures, including a recommendation for the use of force, to meet a situation that endangers the peace of the hemisphere. He referred to Mr. Martin, Assistant Secretary for Latin America, for a judgment about the possibility of getting the necessary two-thirds vote in the O.A.S.

Meeker then addressed the possible argument that O.A.S. action of this kind would amount to 'enforcement action' requiring Security Council authorization under Article 53 of the Charter. He thought there was a reasonably good argument to the contrary. He was not sure that the United States could persuade a majority of the Council to its view, but noted that the veto made it possible to prevent adverse Council action.

Later in the discussion, Mr. Acheson commented that so far as questions of international law might be involved, he agreed with Mr. Katzenbach's position that self-defence was an entirely sufficient justification. He added that if there were to be imported a qualification or requirement of approval by the O.A.S., as apparently suggested by Mr. Meeker, he could not go along with that. Finally, as the meeting recessed for two subgroups to work out detailed scenarios of the alternatives then under consideration, blockade and air strike, the legal aspect was sounded once again. Robert Kennedy, in parting, said that he thought there was ample legal basis for a blockade. Meeker said he was in agreement provided the O.A.S. approved under the Rio Treaty. The Attorney General countered that the O.A.S. action was political not legal. The issue was left in that state. This comment of Robert Kennedy's at the time contrasts with his retrospective evaluation in *Thirteen Days*. There he said 'It was the vote of the Organization of American States that gave a legal basis for the quarantine . . .

It . . . changed our position from that of an outlaw acting in violation of international law into a country acting in accordance with twenty allies legally protecting their position.'[35]

iii

A number of the principals had already been exposed to the relevant legal issues before the Executive Committee meeting of Friday 19 October. In the previous six or eight weeks, the three major departments involved, Justice, State, and Defense, had independently prepared extensive legal memoranda on closely related questions. These memoranda had been reviewed in detail with a number of senior officials who were ultimately involved in the missile crisis.

The first of these analyses was developed in the Department of Justice in late August and was used in the preparation of the President's 4 September press statement quoted above.[36] The Justice Department memorandum is reproduced in full in Appendix I.[37] It was prepared at the express request of Robert Kennedy, by Norbert Schlei, just-appointed Assistant Attorney General, Office of Legal Counsel. According to Mr. Schlei, the Attorney General 'thought that maybe the President ought to issue some sort of warning statement to the Soviet Union so that it would know in advance that we would not tolerate the installation of long-range ballistic missiles'.[38] But before doing so, he 'thought that we ought to do a serious study of whether the United States could as a matter of international law, take action to prevent long-range missiles from being installed in Cuba, and perhaps of what form that action might take . . .'.[39]

The study was completed 'sometime after the middle of August, . . .'.[40] It is divided into two main substantive sections. The first deals with the situation under general international law. It consists primarily of a classical discussion of self-defence and concludes:

[35] Kennedy at 121.
[36] See p. 9 *supra*.
[37] P. 107 *infra*. In addition to the memorandum itself the Appendix reproduces at p. 132 a letter from Mr. Schlei recounting the circumstances of its preparation.
[38] Appendix I at 132.
[39] Ibid.
[40] Ibid.

It is thus clear that preventive action would not ordinarily be lawful to prevent the maintenance of missile bases or other armaments in the absence of evidence that their actual use for an aggressive attack was imminent.[41]

The memorandum adds that membership in international organizations like the U.N. or the O.A.S. 'undoubtedly carries with it a commitment to have recourse to the organization's procedures if at all possible before acting unilaterally'.[42] Finally, the first section points out that 'Both the UN Charter and the Charter of the O.A.S. authorize collective action upon less provocation than would be required to justify unilateral action', citing Article 39 of the Charter and Article 6 of the Rio Treaty.[43]

Section II of the memorandum argues that a special regional legal regime prevails in the western hemisphere.

The historical materials which are appended show that the Monroe Doctrine has from the beginning represented a regional variation in the international law of self-defense. The Doctrine asserts that, in order to insulate the Americas from dangers to peace and security stemming from conflicts involving non-American states, the occupation or control of American territory by a non-American power in itself shall be deemed to present a sufficient danger to warrant exercise by the United States and other American powers of the right of self-defense. The result of the consistent adherence to this attitude by the United States and most other American states, together with the acquiescence of the rest of the civilized world, has been to create a specialized, regional body of law under which preventive action in self-defense is, in the Americas, authorized under less restrictive conditions than would be required in some other regions.[44]

The thrust of the argument is that the emplacement of offensive missiles in Cuba would fall within the 'less restrictive conditions', but the memorandum never expressly comes out and says so. Moreover, it acknowledges that 'traditional legal concepts of

[41] Id. at 109.

[42] Id. at 110.

[43] Ibid. Article 39 empowers the Security Council to 'determine the existence of any threat to the peace' and 'to decide what measures shall be taken . . . to maintain or restore international peace and security'. Article 6 of the Rio Treaty authorizes the Organ of Consultation of the O.A.S., in a 'situation that might endanger the peace of America', to decide on 'the measures which should be taken . . . for the maintenance of the peace and security of the Continent'.

[44] Id. at 111. The historical materials referred to are contained in an Appendix to the memorandum, p. 116. The latest incident included is the stationing of United States forces in Greenland in 1941.

general application do not expressly recognize interests in bloc security', and that 'publicists in the field of international law have not yet formulated concepts and doctrines which expressly recognize the changed world situation'.[45]

Schlei says he discussed the memorandum orally at some length with the Attorney General. The xerox copy made available to me has a hand-written notation indicating that it was sent 'to Dept. State (Rusk)' on 30 August. Schlei thinks it was sent at about the same time to the President, McNamara, Dillon, and possibly to Bundy and McCone. In any event he recalls that Attorney General Kennedy set up a meeting among Katzenbach, Schlei, and Rusk on Labor Day (3 September), 'to discuss the memo and the problem'.[46]

Schlei says the memorandum was accompanied by a draft of a Presidential statement, which was apparently the basis of a discussion in the White House on 4 September. Revised, probably quite drastically, by Bundy with others chiming in, it became the press statement that day in which the President first distinguished between offensive and defensive missiles in Cuba.[47] Robert Kennedy, referring to the 4 September statement in his book, says that it was based on a 'draft prepared by Nicholas Katzenbach, the Deputy Attorney General, and myself'.[48]

In the State Department, the Legal Adviser's Office did not address the missile issue itself in advance of the event. But it had been at work on closely related matters. In late September, as already noted, a decision was taken to suspend U-2 overflights over the western part of Cuba.[49] Secretary Rusk asked me to investigate the possibilities of renewing these flights under the auspices of the O.A.S., as a way of legitimizing them and reducing the political consequences if a U-2 should be brought down.

A legal memorandum responding to this request, prepared in the last few days of September, is included as Appendix II.[50] By and large it covers the same issues that were treated in the legal memorandum distributed by the State Department when

---

[45] Id. at 113.   [46] Id. at 133.   [47] See p. 9 *supra*.
[48] Kennedy at 26.   [49] See p. 12 *supra*.
[50] The text reprinted in the Appendix is from my personal files. After a discussion of the issues with the Secretary, it was decided to abandon the idea of requesting an O.A.S. resolution to authorize the overflights. See p. 21 *infra*. Consequently, the memorandum was never placed in final form and forwarded through channels. See pp. 20–1 *infra*, and n. 56 *infra*.

the quarantine was imposed six weeks later.[51] A comparison of the two documents shows that the structure of the analysis and the order of presentation is the same in each.

The September memorandum concludes that the situation then existing could fairly be characterized by the Organ of Consultation as one threatening the peace of America within the meaning of Article 6 of the Rio Treaty. This would provide a predicate for O.A.S. action under that article, though not under Article 3, which deals exclusively with cases of armed attack. Surveillance overflights, it was argued, could be brought within the catalogue of measures the Organ was empowered to take in such cases under Article 8 of the Treaty.[52]

The memorandum then addresses the question whether the resolution of the O.A.S. Meeting of Foreign Ministers in January 1962, declaring the exclusion of 'the present government of Cuba from participation in the inter-American system', operated to divest or limit the power of the Organ of Consultation. The discussion on this point is much fuller and a good deal more explicit than any official statement. It recognizes the appeal of the argument that 'the O.A.S. could not deprive Cuba of the benefits and privileges of the inter-American system and still hold her to the burdens and restrictions on the ordinary scope of sovereign rights'.[53] But it stresses that the O.A.S. did not purport to expel Cuba from the organization and that Cuba itself had not denounced or withdrawn from any of the relevant treaties.[54]

Finally, the memorandum considers the nexus between regional action and the United Nations via Article 2(4) and Article 53 of the U.N. Charter. It advances the view that overflight is not a 'use of force' within the meaning of Article 2(4).[55]

The overflight memorandum was not sent forward officially but I reviewed it personally with the Secretary. The conclusion of the analysis was that, although in the circumstances the Organ of Consultation had the power to authorize overflights of Cuba, it was not clear that this authorization would necessarily limit Cuba's right to take counter-measures. Partly for this reason,

---

[51] See Appendix III and discussion pp. 48–62 *infra*. A major point of difference is that the significance of the exclusion of Cuba from participation in the organs of the O.A.S. is discussed in the overflight memorandum but not in the later one.

[52] Appendix II at 136–7.   [53] Id. at 137.

[54] Ibid.   [55] Id. at 138.

partly because of the difficulty of securing a timely favourable vote in the O.A.S., and partly from a concern that public consideration of the matter might be taken by the Soviets as a challenge, the project was abandoned. Instead, for what it was worth politically, a reference was included in the communiqué of a meeting of Latin American foreign ministers held in Washington on October 2 and 3:

The meeting observed that it is desirable to intensify the individual and collective surveillance of the delivery of arms and implements of war and all other items of strategic importance to the Communist regime of Cuba . . .[56]

Finally, the General Counsel's Office in the Department of Defense had also considered the legal issues in advance. An opinion dated 14 September, 1962 reads in 'pertinent part' as follows:

. . . the use of such a measure would not be permissible under the United Nations Charter unless: (1) the Security Council had found the existence of a threat to the peace and had recommended measures, including a naval blockade, in accordance with Articles 39, 41 and 42 of the Charter, (2) such action were, pursuant to Article 51, taken on the basis of individual or collective self-defense because of armed attack, or (3) such action were taken as a result of a decision by the O.A.S.

With regard to alternative (3) above all members of the O.A.S., besides agreeing not to have recourse to the use of force, are bound to submit all international disputes that may arise to the Organ of Consultation of the Inter-American System. The Organ of Consultation, like the Security Council, may recommend the taking of certain measures, including a belligerent blockade, to deal with a threat to the peace which is found to exist.[57]

---

[56] *N.Y. Times*, 4 Oct. 1962, p. 10, col. 5. A reference to this action was included in President Kennedy's Report to the American People on the Soviet Arms Buildup in Cuba. [1962] *Public Papers of the Presidents, John F. Kennedy* 806. A position paper prepared for the meeting of 2–3 October recommended that '[t]he U.S. should initiate discussion of, disseminate an understanding of, and utilize the occasion of the meeting to prepare the groundwork as to the desirability of holding a meeting of Foreign Ministers under Article 6 of the Rio Treaty to agree upon a "right to overflight" under Article 8 of that Treaty', Dept. of State, Meeting with Latin American Foreign Ministers: Position Paper, 1 (2 Oct. 1962).

[57] Letter from Mr. Benjamin Forman, Assistant General Counsel for International Affairs, Department of Defense, to Professor Abram Chayes dated 16 Feb. 1971.

The three memoranda are illustrative of the variety of ways in which law and lawyers can get a foot in the door to policy-making. As the President's brother and confidant, Robert Kennedy was assured of a place in the councils of decision. But there are values in participating as of right, by virtue of one's official responsibility. It is not too difficult for the lawyer who wants access to a policy decision to discover legal problems about the courses proposed. Robert Kennedy's request for 'an international law work-up' at the Department of Justice appears to be a typical example of this kind of legal imperialism in operation.

The Defense Department memorandum, on the other hand, appears to be the product of comprehensive staff work. The military were, presumably, engaged in contingency planning. The standard procedure calls for a legal opinion. The lawyers were consulted and duly produced one. It took its place among the required supporting documents for the contingency plan.

In the State Department, neither the Secretary himself nor the bureaucratic routine was so likely to generate a reference to the Legal Adviser. There, the missiles in Cuba were seen as presenting issues predominantly political in content. On such matters, the foreign service tends to share Mr. Kennan's bias and to think of lawyers as basically intermeddlers in a situation that calls for flexible *ad hoc* response. The Secretary, or at least Secretary Rusk, characteristically dealt with the offices having direct-line responsibility for action, which, in a case like this, would be the geographical bureaux concerned. The Legal Adviser's views were requested only when a matter arose in which he would have similar direct-line responsibility: the effect of a resolution of an international organization under its Charter.

Whatever their origins, the memoranda exhibit differences in approach, workmanship, and result that are typical of the profession:

. . . the lawyer rarely looks for or expects ιo find clear answers. More often than not, he searches his data base—treatises, articles, statutes, cases, and other materials—in order to construct legally acceptable arguments in pursuit of one or more objectives.[58]

The largest doctrinal departure from common ground among the three memoranda is the Justice Department's argument for a

[58] Buchanan and Headrick, 'Some Speculation About Artificial Intelligence and Legal Reasoning', 23 Stan. L. Rev. 40 (1971).

special hemispheric law. This position did not surface again in the policy debate. Schlei, discussing the 4 September meeting in the White House, says that

... The President was critical of our draft [statement] because it mentioned the Monroe Doctrine. 'The Monroe Doctrine,' he snapped at me, 'What the hell is that?' I mumbled some answer about its legal significance, but it was clear that whatever it was or meant, he didn't want to mention it in his statement.[59]

The President, in this case perhaps a better lawyer than the professionals, buried the Doctrine as a basis for the claim of a special hemispheric legal regime. Although his speech on 22 October contains a reference to 'the tradition of this Nation and hemisphere',[60] neither the quarantine Proclamation[61] nor, *a fortiori*, the O.A.S. resolution mentions the Doctrine.[62] Katzenbach's statement to the Executive Committee that from the standpoint of international law United States action could be justified on the principle of self-defence seems to have been made without reference to the concept of a special legal regime for the Americas.

On the other hand, there is a very broad area of agreement among the lawyers. All three memoranda hold that under general international law, the mere emplacement of ground-to-ground missiles in Cuba was not an armed attack warranting use of force in self-defence. All agree that the O.A.S. could authorize such a response under Article 6 of the Rio Treaty, even without an armed attack. And all suggest, with varying degrees of

---

[59] Appendix I at 133. The President's instinct was sound. Although the idea of a special regime of law for the western hemisphere, based on the Monroe Doctrine, has sometimes been advanced by United States legal scholars, see, e.g. the authorities cited in Appendix I, it has not been embraced by any other western hemisphere publicist. Whatever substance there may once have been to the United States claim of a special prerogative in the hemisphere can hardly have survived the multilateral treaties concluded after the Second World War to govern hemispheric relations. See Charter of the Organization of American States, 30 Apr. 1948, [1951] 2 U.S.T. 2394, 119 U.N.T.S. 3 (effective 13 Dec. 1951), especially Articles 15–19; Inter-American Treaty of Reciprocal Assistance, 2 Sept. 1947, 62 Stat. 1681 (1948), 21 U.N.T.S. 77 (effective 3 Dec. 1948). It is difficult to believe that in 1962 unilateral action by the United States premissed on the Monroe Doctrine, would have been greeted with enthusiasm by other nations in the hemisphere.

[60] [1962] *Public Papers of the Presidents, John F. Kennedy* 806.

[61] Proclamation No. 3504, 23 Oct. 1962, 27 Fed. Reg. 10, 401 (1962).

[62] OEA/Ser. 6/V/C-d-1024, Annex A (1962).

emphasis, an obligation to consult the O.A.S., and perhaps the U.N., before taking unilateral action.

To sum up, the legal officers of the cabinet departments chiefly concerned had examined in detail the international legal questions involved in the United States response to the emplacement of missiles in Cuba well before the event, but in the context of the developing crisis. Working independently, they had reached a remarkably consistent view of those issues. This analysis was maintained with little variation throughout the crisis period, and provided the main elements of the public legal defence of the quarantine once the decision was announced.

The legal conclusions did not remain gathering dust in lawyers' files. They were thoroughly reviewed with the Department heads in the weeks immediately preceding the discovery of the missiles in Cuba, and probably were seen by other senior officials as well. There is no reason to doubt that most of the members of the Executive Committee were generally familiar with the legal background and issues. When the missiles were discovered, the memoranda were in being as physical artifacts. The legal arguments were there, available for whatever use might be made of them by one or another participant or faction, grist for the mill of decision.

III

LAW AS CONSTRAINT: THE CHOICE OF THE QUARANTINE

i

MOST people, layman and lawyers alike, typically think of law as a prohibition, a thou-shalt-not. It is a set of rules proscribing certain conduct—whether it be coveting thy neighbour's wife or exceeding the speed-limit—with penalties or sanctions attached to violation. Whether from a desire to avoid the sanction or otherwise, conduct is brought into compliance with the applicable rule or norm. Non-complying conduct is constrained.

A little reflection shows that this is only a partial, and on the whole distorting, view of the legal system.[1] Even where the object of the law is to avoid or minimize certain kinds of behaviour, outright prohibition is by no means the commonest device employed. Very often it is not effective even if it is used, as is demonstrated by the experience with criminal laws against the use of drugs or alchohol. The legal system promotes or discourages conduct by a subtle intermixture of a broad range of inducements and penalties. It allocates benefits and burdens, opportunities and risks, often in ways whose relation to the activity to be influenced seems remote or subterranean.[2]

Even more important, whole areas of the law, of increasing importance in modern times, are hardly concerned at all with prohibiting or encouraging particular kinds of conduct. The law of contract is a pervasive example of this type. Formally, and in good part substantively as well, it is a matter of indifference from the point of view of the law whether one chooses to enter into

[1] Recent years have seen a growing body of jurisprudential literature rejecting this simplistic normative conception of law. My own greatest debt for broader insights is to the late Professor Henry Hart. See Hart and Sacks, *The Legal Process: Basic Problems in the Making and Application of Law* (temporary ed., 1958). The authors' views are summarized at 1–9. See also Fuller, *The Morality of Law* 152–86 (1964). Similar ideas are applied to the international-law field in Henkin, *How Nations Behave* (1968), especially at 13–23.

[2] Schelling, 'On the Ecology of Micromotives', *The Public Interest* 59 (Fall 1971).

contracts or not. If one does so choose, certain consequences attach; but the choice remains with the actor in a way that it does not for activity covered by criminal or tort law. What the law of contract does, at least in its classical form, is to provide a framework for the self-organizing activities of individuals in pursuit of goals that are broadly speaking, autonomously chosen.[3]

As will appear, the law operated in a number of these essentially facilitative ways in the Cuban missile crisis. But it will not do to evade the more primitive question whether law operated as a constraint, in the sense of narrowing choice or excluding certain courses of action. That question opens up a larger and more difficult one: in what sense and upon what evidence can we say that the conduct or behaviour of a corporate aggregate of the scope and dimensions of a state, is constrained?

We are not even very clear how law operates to channel individual behaviour. For the most part, compliance with law is not felt as a limit upon otherwise desired activity. The process of socialization is, in large part, the process of internalizing legal and other kinds of norms. Moreover, the standards embodied in the legal system of a society are not, on the whole, externally derived and imposed on the members. The law develops in reciprocal interaction with the conduct it is supposed to regulate, so that at any point, the law expresses in marked degree the values and purposes of the society in which it functions. Obedience to law is most often not perceived as response to an external constraint, but as the affirmation of valued and desired objectives.[4]

Secondly, even if conduct violates a relatively determinate legal standard, it does not necessarily follow that the action was unaffected by the law. Do we believe that the behaviour of a man travelling 65 miles an hour on a super-highway with a 60-mile speed-limit was not constrained by law?

[3] II Parsons, The Law of Contracts 1–2 (1855); see Kennedy, Legal Formality, 2 J. Legal Studies, 351, 374–5 and n. 40 (1973). Note that contract law promotes a regime of autonomous choice only to the extent that the assumptions of classical contract theory are operative. The assumptions are roughly parallel to those defining a free competitive market in classical economic theory—and just as unreal in practice. See Friedman and Macaulay, *Law and the Behavioral Sciences* 302, (1969). See also H. L. A. Hart, *The Concept of Law* 25–48 (1961); Hart and Sacks, n. 1 *supra*, at 183–5; 207ff.

[4] See n. 1 *supra*. For a recent generalized view of the interaction between the legal system and economic and social conduct see Steiner, 'Legal Education and Socio-economic Change: Brazilian Perspectives', 19 Am. J. Comp. L. 39 (1971).

Third, in most cases the applicable law is by no means as clear as the speed-limit. In a case of any difficulty, it is not possible to say categorically in advance whether a proposed course of action is 'lawful' or not. Partly this is because legal consequences, especially in the common-law tradition, are very sensitive to nuances of the fact-setting and the concrete details of the challenged activity. These do not emerge until the action is taken. The relevant facts are, in a sense, defined by the action.

The indeterminacy of the law, however, runs deeper than the common human inability to predict the detailed shape of a necessarily contingent future. In principle, under the conventions of the American legal system, no lawyer or collection of lawyers can give a definitive opinion as to the legality of conduct in advance. Only an entity, usually a court, officially empowered for the purpose and duly invoked in accordance with procedures by which it is authorized to act, can give a conclusive answer to a question of legality. Even then, the answer is definitive only for that case and those parties. As every first-year law student quickly discovers, court judgments that have determined controversies and ruined lives can be and often are 'wrong' about what the law is.[5]

Still further contingencies are inherent in the procedures of the court or other decisional agency. Will an aggrieved party be able or willing to invoke those processes and to persist until judgment is given? Even if he does, the result will be predicated not on what happened in the 'real' world, but upon what can be made to appear about the events through the artificial and highly selective investigative procedures of the tribunal. The judgment itself may go off on a side-issue, often a procedural question, that the parties recognize is not central to the challenged conduct.

In these circumstances, it may not be too difficult to advise a client whose aim is to stay out of entanglement with the law at all costs. The legal advice will be not to act. But in most cases the objective of avoiding legal difficulties will not be the primary one, nor should it be. Legal advice must come to the client in the form of an assessment of risks and probabilities, with the client, by and large, making the choice of which he will bear. At some point, this comes perilously close to reducing itself to Holmes's 'bad man' view of the law, which cares for nothing except the unpleasant consequences that will be brought to bear on the actor.[6] Or, more

[5] Hart and Sacks, n. 1 supra, at 4-5.
[6] Holmes, 'The Path of the Law', Collected Legal Papers 167, 169-74, (1920).

neutrally, it suggests the approach of an 'economic man', who will persist in the activity as long as its value to him outweighs its burdens, measured in terms of the size of the penalty times the risk of enforcement.[7] If, after completing his assessment, the client chooses to go forward and the adverse contingencies materialize, will we say that the law has not affected or constrained his conduct?

All these difficulties in understanding the impact of the law on conduct are multiplied many times when the conduct of the state is at issue. For the Romanists, the body corporate 'is incapable of knowing, intending, willing, acting'.[8] And even today, these words can hardly be used of the state without elements of metaphor. They carry the connotation of an actor much more unified and coherent than a national government, and more directly responsive to the motivations and influences, whether of morals or interest, that shape the behaviour of man and woman.

The case before us—the decision for the quarantine—may seem to minimize the difficulties of extrapolation from individual to corporate behaviour. On the surface, it is the very model of the rational process of decision-making that is the unspoken premiss of most analysis of government behaviour in the national security field: a systematic, not overhurried canvass of alternatives and the considerations bearing on choice among them, conducted by a small, fairly homogeneous group of men, agreed in their sense of the gravity and moment of the situation, bound together in political and personal comradeship and in loyalty to the President, to whom alone, as all acknowledged, belonged the final choice.[9] All of the eyewitness accounts agree with Sorensen that

---

[7] Calabresi, *The Cost of Accidents* 119 (1970).

[8] Gierke, *Political Theories of the Middle Age* xx (1958) (Maitland translation). See also Hallis, *Corporate Personality* 8 (1930): 'It has neither will nor self-consciousness. It is a dead form, not a living reality, a concept which can enter into jural relations only so long and in so far as the state breathes into it the vital power of jural capacity. . . . The artificial person which the state creates has no will, no mind, and these the state cannot grant it.' But see Laski, 'The Personality of Associations', 29 Harv. L. Rev. 404 (1916), and Maitland's Introduction to Gierke, *supra*.

[9] Allison at 276. The quarantine decision is often thought to exemplify the terrifying time-pressures under which peace–war decisions must be taken. The Committee saw itself as working against two short deadlines: (1) the moment when the missiles would become operational, which was thought to be about a week after they were discovered, Kennedy at 35 (1969); and (2) the period

... one of the remarkable aspects of those meetings was a sense of complete equality. Protocol mattered little when the nation's life was at stake. Experience mattered little in a crisis which had no precedent. Even rank mattered little when secrecy prevented staff support. We were fifteen individuals on our own, representing the President and not different departments.[10]

No doubt all this was true. But even in this case and in this group, Graham Allison is able to demonstrate convincingly that the force of bureaucratic routine or momentum, the push and pull of political bargaining, profoundly shaped the result.[11] There is no suggestion that the motives of the members of the Committee were self-regarding or unworthy, or indeed that there was anything but an entire regard for the country's welfare as each man saw it. Allison's point is that the differences among the men of the Executive Committee were inherent in the situation—differences in personality and outlook, differences in susceptibility to various considerations, grounded in differences in background and training and experience. Equally significant, perhaps more so, are differences in perspective and perception stemming from the different positions held by the participants, the different responsibilities entailed, the difference in personal and political stakes for each of the men around the table. Members of the Committee themselves acknowledged these differences in outlook. For example, Paul Nitze, in defence of Ambassador Stevenson, said, 'Adlai had to be the one who looked at this proposition from the U.N. standpoint, the standpoint of simple equities and the hazards of war.'[12] And surely it cannot have been entirely coincidental that the strongest proponents of war were the chiefs of the nation's armed services.

Allison, borrowing an aphorism from Donald Price, says that

---

during which the affair could be kept secret, which was, as it turned out, less than a week. But in fact the process consumed an extraordinary number of high-level man-hours in an equally extraordinary concentration. The members of the Executive Commitee worked on Cuba to the exclusion of all other matters for a full week, thus achieving a level of sustained deliberation and personal give and take that was unusual if not unprecedented in national security decision-making.

[10] Sorensen at 679. See also Abel at 58; Kennedy at 46; but cf. Allison at 207.

[11] Allison at 117–32; 187–210.

[12] Abel at 95.

in national security decision-making, 'Where you stand depends on where you sit.'[13]

The 'leaders' who sit on top of organizations are not a monolithic group. Rather, each individual in this group is, in his own right, a player in a central, competitive game. The name of the game is politics: bargaining along regularized circuits among players positioned hierarchically within the government. . . . [T]he Governmental (or Bureaucratic Politics) Model [of government decision-making] sees no unitary actor but rather many actors as players—players who focus not on a single strategic issue but on many diverse intra-national problems as well; players who act in terms of no consistent set of strategic objectives but rather according to various conceptions of national, organizational and personal goals; players who make government decisions not by a single rational choice but by the pulling and hauling that is politics.[14]

Legal considerations—like military or diplomatic or political considerations—operated on decision not directly, but mediately, filtered through the different purposes, perspectives, and susceptibilities of the players in the central game.

ii

The 19 October session of the Executive Committee described above[15] is an illuminating instance of one round in a game such as Allison describes. It is of obvious importance for this study, because it is the round in which legal considerations were most prominently in play.

For most of the participants in that session, the lawfulness of United States action was not their special concern, their reason for being there. For Meeker it was. His focus was predictable for those who knew him. He had a deep personal commitment to the application of law in international affairs, and an idealism about its possibilities, that fifteen years' service in the State Department had not been able to suppress. His experience supported a generous view of the capacities of international organizations. For many years, he had worked on legal affairs of the United Nations. In particular, he had been heavily involved in 1950 in the development of the Uniting for Peace Resolution, which authorized the

---

[13] Allison at 176.
[14] Id. at 144.
[15] See pp. 14–17 *supra*.

General Assembly to carry forward the Korean operation after the Soviets ended their boycott of the Security Council.[16]

Added to these personal qualities were the bureaucratic exigencies of 'where he sat'. He was, at that moment, Acting Legal Adviser, the officially responsible custodian of the legal interest of the State Department. We may concede that considerations of bureaucratic prerogative were not foremost or even consciously in his mind. Nevertheless, it remains a fact that, to the extent legal considerations could be brought to bear on the decision, the position of the Office of Legal Adviser in the Department and, more importantly, the subsequent role of the Office in the development and execution of the decision would be enhanced. Moreover, whatever the decision, the responsibility would fall to that Office to make the legal defence of the action before both the public and professional colleagues. At the same time, Meeker was relatively junior in rank among those present, and he appeared in the traditional role of the lawyer as a staff rather than line officer. He could be confident that if he concentrated on the law, there were those who would see to it that other interests and other factors were not overlooked.

Meeker knew, of course, that the highest priority for his auditors and his ultimate client, the President, was not to stay out of legal trouble at all costs. Thus, he could not counsel passivity. His function had to be to provide a fair assessment of the legal possibilities and risks of the courses that were under consideration. Within that framework his own policy orientation led him to take the most restrictive view of the legal situation. In particular, he took the categorical position that the missile emplacement could not be regarded as an armed attack,[17] although, as a practical no less than a legal matter, the President could not have ordered unilateral action without publicly characterizing the threat in these terms. Moreover, although Meeker did not expressly limit

[16] Uniting for Peace, G. A. Res. 377 (V) (3 Nov. 1950), GAOR 347 (5th Sess. 1950). At the time of the invasion of South Korea in June 1950, the Soviet Union was boycotting the meetings of the Council. The Security Council was able to take action without concern about a Soviet veto. After the U.N. operation had begun, the Soviets decided to resume attendance, and this rendered the Security Council ineffective as a directive and legitimating organ for U.N. action. Thus the need for some way of transferring responsibility to another entity. See Woolsey, 'The "Uniting for Peace" Resolution of the United Nations', 45 Am. J. Int'l L. 129 (1951).

[17] See n. 34, p. 15 *supra*, and discussion, p. 15 *supra*.

the scope of the analysis, his conclusion was that the O.A.S. could legitimate a 'defensive quarantine',[18] and the question of harsher steps was left open. This implicit qualification does not appear in any of the earlier legal memoranda, except as it may instance the general requirement of proportionality in all 'defensive' action.[19]

The difference between these views and Mr. Katzenbach's exposition are also illuminated by Allison's analytical framework. Mr. Katzenbach's position can be taken as reflecting the concerns and perspective of Robert Kennedy. By this time, the Attorney General had emerged as the chief advocate of a decision for a blockade as opposed to an air strike, the only alternative that was still viable.[20] Both Kennedy and Katzenbach were fully conversant with the earlier Justice Department memorandum emphasizing the difficulties of unilateral action and the importance of O.A.S. approval from a legal point of view.[21] We may add to this Kennedy's hindsight acknowledgement that 'It was the vote of the Organization of American States that gave a legal basis for the quarantine.'[22] Why then did the Attorney General resist the legal analysis that provided the strongest support for the policy position he was advocating?

Kennedy sat at that table not only as the chief legal officer of the government (although his insistence that Katzenbach and Justice speak first shows that he was conscious of that primacy). He was, in Macmillan's words, the President's 'adjutant'.[23] He knew that, although the President too was leaning strongly towards a blockade, the final decision had not yet been made, and the choice of more forceful action might yet be taken. Moreover, there is evidence that he was sensitive to the political risks of an

[18] See n. 33, p. 14 *supra*, and discussion, p. 16 *supra*.

[19] Appendix I at 109, McDougal, 'The Soviet–Cuban Quarantine and Self-Defense', 57 Am. J. Int'l L. 597, 603 n. 14 (1963). See also Henkin, *How Nations Behave* 230 (1968). Henkin argues that the quarantine, unlike air strike or blockade, may not have been a use of force within Article 2(4). Id. at 238–9. But this argument may prove too much, for if that conclusion is accepted, a blockade or quarantine would have been permissible even if unilaterally imposed by the United States without O.A.S. approval. See pp. 151–2 *infra*.

[20] Kennedy at 14–15 (Introduction by Robert S. McNamara) and at 38–9; Abel at 64–5; Allison at 197; Hilsman at 203.

[21] Appendix I, p. 110; see p. 16 *supra*.

[22] Kennedy at 121.

[23] Id. at 17 (Introduction by Harold Macmillan).

unsuccessful appeal to the O.A.S. He said at the meeting that the President would be put in an impossible position if he went to the O.A.S. and it failed to approve the action, or even if there were a substantial delay.[24] For the President's adjutant, it was vital that both the option of stronger action and the option of unilateral action should not be foreclosed until the President had made his own choice, and made it in the light of *all* the considerations, legal and non-legal, bearing on action. Katzenbach's legal analysis fits this purpose.

The others, too, responded from where they sat. Acheson was without any official responsibility, much less responsibility for the defence of the legality of action. Of all the participants, he was the only one who could and did leave when his advice was rejected.[25] Like the Attorney General, but with a much narrower purpose, he was concerned that the choice of an air strike should not appear to be foreclosed by legal restraints. His position was categorical. He committed his prestige both as lawyer and as former Secretary to the proposition that the limitations put forward by Meeker were misconceived. Beyond that, he disparaged the legal problem, dismissing the legal issues as not worthy of serious consideration. No doubt this reflected his honest judgment. He maintained his position with unbroken consistency and undiminished vigour until his death.[26] Why then was it necessary for him to answer at all? Why not save his ammunition for a worthier target? Acheson's intervention can be seen not only as an expression of conviction, but as the behaviour to be expected from an air strike proponent with his credentials. Meeker's legal argument, like any other kind of argument, would carry weight with some of the group. Blockade advocates would inevitably cite it in support of their position. Like any other opposing argument, therefore—military, political, diplomatic—

[24] See n. 34, p. 15 *supra*.

[25] After he realized that the decision would be against an air strike, Acheson returned to his Maryland farm and did not continue to participate in the ExCom meetings. Since he was not an official of the government, he did not believe he should help draft plans for the quarantine he had opposed. Abel at 88–9; Allison at 207–8. He returned the following week to do service as the President's personal emissary to Gen. de Gaulle and Chancellor Adenauer. See p. 75 *infra*.

[26] See remarks of Acheson in [1963] Proc. Am. Soc. Int'l L. 13, 14; Acheson, 'Dean Acheson's Version of Robert Kennedy's Version of the Cuban Missile Affair', *Esquire* (Feb. 1969).

it was not to be ignored but answered, by the force of personality and prestige as well as by reason.

Thompson stressed the legalistic streak in the Russians, and the importance therefore of being able to present a strong legal case in defence of United States action. Martin, the Assistant Secretary for Latin America, had, like Meeker, a bureaucratic interest in an expanded O.A.S. role. In response to the Attorney General's concern, described above, he tried to assure the group that reference to the O.A.S. was feasible in practice. He thought that the United States could get the needed fourteen votes, and perhaps three or four more with an approach to Latin American heads of state. Given the weight that Robert Kennedy attached to the question of the O.A.S. response, Martin put himself pretty far out on a limb.[27]

And so it went with others, too, no doubt, who made no comment. Each pursued his own purpose and vision, not parochial, but slightly different from the others, within the collective framework. Each tended his own garden, incorporating into it—whether for decorative purposes or more substantial reasons, whether much or little—what he drew from the legal debate he heard.

The purpose of this discussion is not to praise or criticize the members of the Executive Committee, still less to rate them on a scale from 'lawful' to 'Machiavellian'. It is to demonstrate that a differential response to legal considerations inevitably emerges from the differing positions, responsibilities, and tactics of the participants in the process of collective decision. If Meeker was more concerned for the legal aspects, this reflects not superior morality but the focus of his responsibility. From the perspective of others, different considerations had to be stressed, although not necessarily to the exclusion of legal factors.

Neither the extended discussion of legal matters in the Executive Committee nor the differential response is unusual or, on reflection, surprising. Both are inherent in the nature of decision-making as an interplay among men with different positions, perceptions, strategies, and stakes, and in the nature of law as an indeterminate datum rather than a categoric norm. Given these

[27] See n. 34, p. 15 *supra*. Abel says Martin's estimate was 'that with luck, the blockade would get fourteen approving votes, the bare minimum required'. Abel at 129. But Meeker's recollection of the meeting contradicts this, and it is hard to believe the President would have accepted the risks of the O.A.S. on such a pessimistic prognosis. See pp. 67–8 *infra*.

two realities, it is almost impossible that legal considerations should *not* enter the process of decision. They will always tend to favour one or more of the players in the game, who will see that they are brought to bear. That a case of primary causation cannot be established is no more fatal to the operation of legal factors than of any other kind of indeterminate data or analysis bearing on decision.[28]

iii

The foregoing discussion might be taken as a sufficient answer to the question whether law operated as a constraint on the choice of the quarantine as the United States response in the Cuban missile crisis. One can conclude that it did, and substantially, but not decisively, and not directly in the sense that the President, or anyone else, turned to his lawyer and said, 'I am disposed to do thus-and-so, which I think to be in the best interests of the country, but if you tell me it would be illegal, I won't do it.'

That of course, is caricature. But, I think it can be shown that law, or something very like it, constrained decision in a sense that is close to this stereotype.

One important piece of evidence for constraint would be to examine the conduct in terms of the asserted prohibition. If the conduct complies, there is at least a prima facie argument that the norm operated in its intended sense. The converse is even more compelling: if the conduct violates the norm, it would seem to be very strong evidence that the law did not constrain. And that is the basic structure of the argument of those who contend that the United States ignored international legal norms in the missile crisis. Quincy Wright stated the position forcefully only a few months after the events:

. . . the United States, by the quarantine of October 22, 1962, resorted to a unilateral, forcible action, which cannot be reconciled with its

---

[28] In *The Policy Making Process* (1968), Professor Charles E. Lindblom propounds a similar framework for the impact of 'policy analysis' on actual decisions. This framework is also indeterminate. '[I]nventive as man has been in extending his analytical capacities, he cannot follow through to a conclusive analysis of the merits of alternative policies.' Id. at 116. Thus, policy analysis becomes 'an instrument or weapon in this play of power. . . . It does not avoid fighting over policy; it is a method of fighting.' Id. at 30, 34.

obligations under the United Nations Charter to settle its international disputes by peaceful means and to refrain from use or threat of force in international relations (Article 2, paragraphs 3, 4), except for individual or collective self-defense against armed attack (Article 51), under authority of the United Nations (Article 24, 39), or on invitation of the state where the force is to be used (Article 2, paragraph 1).

The latter exception may apply in respect to Cuba, because it had consented by the Rio and O.A.S. treaties to the use of sanctioning methods against itself if recommended by the Consultative Organ of the Organization of American States. . . .

The quarantine, however, deprived the Soviet Union of its right to 'freedom of the seas.' The United States has always insisted that a 'pacific blockade' may not be applied against the vessels of a third state. The quarantine was a threat contemplating the use of force against the 'political independence' of the Soviet Union to enjoy the right of a state to navigate the high seas in time of peace, and against the purposes of the United Nations to maintain international peace and bring about the peaceful settlement of international disputes.[29]

In summary, the norm, Article 2(4), proscribes the threat or use of force in international affairs (with exceptions not here relevant). The quarantine was a threat or use of force. *Ergo*, the United States action violated the norm. It follows also that the decision was not constrained by the norm: Q.E.D.

Putting aside for the moment the question of the applicability of the exceptions, the power of the syllogism depends on its middle term, that the quarantine was a threat or use of force. In the dictionary meaning of the words, of course, it was. The men who took the decision and the men who manned the ships knew that they were deploying familiar naval forces in a traditional way, under circumstances in which there was a considerable possibility that the armed force the vessels disposed of would be used to coerce the will of Russian ship-captains on the high seas. Both Mr. Meeker's exposition in the Executive Committee[30] and the Department of State Memorandum on The Legal Basis for the

---

[29] Wright, 'The Cuban Quarantine,' [1963] Proc. Am. Soc. Int'l L. 9. See also Wright, 'The Cuban Quarantine', 57 Am. J. Int'l L. 546 (1963); Campbell, 'The Cuban Crisis and the UN Charter: An Analysis of the United States Position', 16 Stan. L. Rev. 160 (1963); Partan, 'The Cuban Quarantine: Some Implications for Self-Defense', [1963] Duke L. J. 696; and Standard, 'The United States Quarantine of Cuba and the Rule of Law', 49 ABA J. 744 (1963).

[30] See p. 15 *supra*.

Quarantine of Cuba proceed on the footing that the threat or use of force was involved.[31]

Nevertheless, the characterization of the quarantine as a prohibited threat of force within the meaning of Article 2(4) is not completely satisfying. Professor Henkin, by no means a fire-eater, argues that it was not,[32] because not directed 'against the territorial integrity or political independence of any state, or in any other manner inconsistent, with the purposes of the United Nations'.[33]

For the purposes of this analysis, we need only recognize the doubt, we need not resolve it. We need not ask whether, if we sat as a court to construe the phrase in a case that properly called for it, we would or should treat the concept of 'threat or use of force' as covering the quarantine. Indeed we should not ask the question in that form, for there is no tribunal that can resolve the issue categorically, and to act 'as if' there were is itself to distort the issue.[34] We need not even ask what is a much more legitimate question: should we as scholars conclude that the system would be well served by a concept of the norm that would include such manifestations as the quarantine in the circumstances in which it was employed? I do not maintain that it would be very easy to refute an affirmative answer to that question. We know, after all, that the Framers of the Charter intended some expansion of the prohibitions on use of force beyond the classical cases of aggression.[35]

---

[31] Appendix III at 143, 148.

[32] Henkin, n. 19 *supra* at 238-9 (1968); see also pp. 152-3 *infra*.

[33] U.N. Charter, Art. 2(4).

[34] Although the I.C.J. has held that any question of Charter interpretation :a 'legal question', *Certain Expenses of the United Nations*, [1962] I.C.J. 151, 165, it is difficult to imagine that the Court would treat the issues raised by the missiles and the quarantine as justiciable even if it could require the parties to submit to its jurisdiction. And, of course, there is no basis for compulsory jurisdiction. The U.S.S.R. has not accepted it, *see* Hague Int. Ct. Just., *Yearbook 1969-1970* 51-80 (1970), and the United States' consent may be qualified or negated by the Connally Reservation, S. Res. 196, 79th Cong., 2nd Sess., 92 Cong. Rec. 10,706 (1946). See *Switzerland* v. *United States*, Interhandel Case (interim measures of protection) Order of 24 Oct. 1957, [1957] I.C.J. 105, 117 (sep. opinion of Judge Sir H. Lauterpacht).

[35] See Russell, *A History of the United Nations Charter* 669-75 (1958). Early in the San Francisco debates the United States representative argued that 'it seemed undesirable to include too narrow a concept of aggression in the Charter. He pointed out that in the future there would be many kinds of aggression and

For present purposes, however, the relevant question is what is the core meaning of the concept 'threat or use of force'. If the Framers were like others who have sought to guide the future, their minds were conditioned and guided by the past. What were the classic instances of threat or use of force in international affairs in their experience? Invasion, sudden and unprovoked or at least greatly disproportionate to the provocation, as in Belgium in 1914 or in Poland in 1939. Air strike without warning, as at Pearl Harbor in 1941.

As the issues presented themselves to the Executive Committee, the alternative to the quarantine was not to do nothing. Rightly or wrongly, that had been ruled out.[36] The alternative to block-ade was precisely either an invasion or an air strike.[37] All accounts of the Executive Committee deliberations agree in attributing primary significance to Robert Kennedy's insistence that the members face up to the comparison with earlier instances of aggression.[38] His first recorded reaction, a scribbled note at the first Executive Committee meeting, was: 'I now know how Tojo felt when he was planning Pearl Harbor.'[39] On Wednesday 17 October, George Ball made the first sustained argument against the air-strike proposal, maintaining that it was inconsistent with United States traditions. Robert Kennedy seconded him saying 'My brother is not going to be the Tojo of the 1960's.'[40] In *Thirteen Days*, Kennedy himself states the argument more fully:

With some trepidation, I argued that, whatever validity the military and political arguments were for an attack in preference to a blockade, America's traditions and history would not permit such a course of action. Whatever military reasons he and others could marshal, they were nevertheless, in the last analysis, advocating a surprise attack by a very large nation against a very small one. This, I said, could not be undertaken by the U.S. if we were to maintain our moral position at home and around the globe. Our struggle against Communism throughout

---

that these would be covered in the Charter by the words "threat to peace".' U.N.C.I.O., *Documents*, vol. 6, 344 (1945).

[36] Allison at 193–5, 202.

[37] Id. at 200.

[38] Id. at 197; Kennedy at 14–15 (Introduction by Robert McNamara); Abel at 64; Hilsman at 203–4, 206; and Sorensen at 684.

[39] Kennedy at 31.

[40] Abel at 64. Allison points out that once the Attorney General had made this comparison, it was hard even for the President to reject it. Allison at 203.

the world was far more than physical survival—it had as its essence our heritage and our ideals, and these we must not destroy.[41]

One might be disposed to attribute a good bit of this passage to the pardonable elaboration of hindsight, except that it parallels very closely contemporaneous accounts of the Executive Committee meetings.[42] Robert McNamara's summary of the argument is also similar:

... he opposed a massive surprise attack by a large country on a small country because he believed such an attack to be inhuman, contrary to our traditions and ideals, and an act of brutality for which the world would never forgive us.[43]

All the accounts agree that the issues thus raised were among the decisive ones. Robert Kennedy says:

We spent more time on this moral question during the first five days than on any other single matter.... We struggled and fought with one another and with our consciences, for it was a question that deeply troubled us all.[44]

'What changed my mind,' said Douglas Dillon, 'was Bobby Kennedy's argument that we ought to be true to ourselves as Americans, that surprise attack was not in our tradition. Frankly, these considerations had not occurred to me until Bobby raised them so eloquently.'[45]

Here is a scene not so very different from what I suggested above might be considered a caricature: responsible, hard-headed, even cynical statesmen facing the conclusion that a proposed course of action might be militarily and politically sound, but arguing or persuaded that it should be rejected because it transgressed a deeply ingrained moral norm.

It is true that the norm was adduced as a moral not a legal one. It is still so regarded in retrospective accounts of the decision. No one stood up and said 'And besides, in addition to being immoral, an air strike is the very kind of conduct forbidden by Article 2(4).' But it is hard to believe that men as familiar as these with the law in general and the specific international-law

[41] Kennedy at 38–9.
[42] See Abel at 64.
[43] Kennedy at 15 (Introduction by Robert McNamara).
[44] Id. at 39.
[45] Abel at 80–1.

context of the situation before them could have been unaware or even unmindful of the legal overtones of the moral proposition. Whatever the general relationship between law and morals, it seems to me that at the level of the use of force in the classic sense, as at the level of homicide in domestic law, legal norm and moral precept are two expressions of the same deep human imperative.[46] It does little justice to ourselves or to the men who 'struggled and fought with one another and with [their] own consciences' to try to package the two aspects into neat, analytically separate components.

If we ask the question what is the minimum Article 2(4) can be held to cover, the answer will be that at the very least it is a rule against aggression and surprise attack. Taken in this sense, and given the alternatives as they were presented to the responsible actors, we may fairly conclude that the rule of Article 2(4) was a significant factor in determining the decision against air strike or invasion and for the lesser measure of a quarantine.

---

[46] See Henkin, n. 19 *supra*, at 223; Oliver, 'International Law and the Quarantine of Cuba: A Hopeful Prescription for Legal Writing', 57 Am. J. Int'l L. 373, 374 (1963).

IV

LAW AS JUSTIFICATION: THE REFERENCE TO THE O.A.S.

i

WHEN it is said that international law is used as 'justification' or 'mere justification' for action, the connotation is that this is illegitimate or at least unworthy—a concern, as one commentator says, 'with wrapping . . . policies in the mantle of legal rectitude'.[1] The legal analysis is seen as something cooked up after the event, by lawyers who had no part in the decision, to justify a course of action chosen essentially on other grounds. International law 'does not have a valid life of its own; it is a mere instrument available to political leaders for their own ends, be they good or evil, peaceful or aggressive'.[2] The words evoke the familiar image of the devious, fork-tongued lawyer, who can and usually does make the worse appear the better cause.

The disparagement of law as 'mere' justification reveals a failure to understand the functions of this kind of 'rationalization' in legal systems in general, and especially in international law. To turn for a moment to the work of domestic courts, the ordinary judicial opinion does not recapitulate the actual process by which the court reached its decision, much less the underlying psychological motivation of individual judges. We recognize that the decisions of courts, which are legal decisions in the purest sense, are inevitably reached on a variety of grounds of interest or policy, as well as, or often quite apart from, legal ratiocination.[3] That does not mean, however, that the judicial opinions filling the law books are a sham. The requirement of a published opinion imposes on the court the discipline and check of the necessity to formulate its decision in terms of the set of legal rules and pro-

---

[1] Gerberding, 'International Law and the Cuban Missile Crisis', in Scheinman and Wilkinson (eds.), *International Law and Political Crisis* 175, 176 (1969).

[2] Id. at 209.

[3] See Cardozo, *The Nature of the Judicial Process* 9–13, 167–78 (1921); Frank, *Law and the Modern Mind* 100–17 (1936); Llewelyn, *The Common Law Tradition: Deciding Appeals* 56–9, 203–6 (1960).

cedures within which the case is presented for determination.[4] Professional critique of an opinion ordinarily proceeds in terms of whether it 'justifies' the decision in an intellectually satisfying way, taking into account the canons, traditions, materials, and leeways of judicial reasoning, or whether on the contrary it is a perfunctory or superficial exercise.[5]

The judicial opinion cannot prove that the decision is right. The court's answer is final on the legal issues only because the tribunal is authoritatively empowered for this purpose.[6] Nor can professional opinion settle the question once and for all, even if it were unanimous, which, given the nature of legal materials, is very unlikely. But, if there can be no determinate answer, analysis and criticism can nevertheless distinguish a persuasive from a specious rationale, a responsible and serious performance from a trivial one. In this way, the requirement of justification provides an important substantive check on the legality of action and ultimately on the responsibility of the decision-making process.

In the field of executive action, domestic or international, justification is not a formal requirement, as it is for judicial decision. But it can and often does play much the same role of showing that the decision is reconcilable with a generally accepted set of norms arguably applicable to the case. The failure to issue a legal opinion at the time of the Cambodian invasion in May 1970 became a significant ground of attack on the propriety of that action.[7] It was rightly taken as presumptive evidence that legal considerations had *not* been adequately reviewed and that legal advice had *not* been adequately consulted. Ultimately, this criticism resulted in the preparation and presentation of full-scale legal opinions both by the Legal Adviser and the Assistant Attorney General, Office of Legal Counsel,[8] which could be and were

---

[4] See Llewelyn, n. 3. *supra*, at 56–9; Hart, 'The Aims of the Criminal Law', 23 L. & Contemp. Prob. 401, 429–30 (1958).

[5] Llewelyn, n. 3. *supra*, at 56–9, 62–120.

[6] See Jackson, J., dissenting, in *Brown* v. *Allen*, 344 U.S. 443, 532 at 540 (1952).

[7] See 'Hammarskjold Forum: Expansion of the Viet Nam War Into Cambodia—the Legal Issues', 45 N.Y.U.L. Rev. 625 (1970); 'The Legal Basis for U.S. Role in Conflict in Cambodia', *N.Y. Times*, 1 May 1970, p. 4, col. 3; 'Symposium on United States Military Action in Cambodia', 65 Am. J. Int'l L. 1 (1971).

[8] Rehnquist, 'The Constitutional Issues—Administration Position', 45

exposed to professional criticism. More important, an internal memorandum in the State Department enjoined fuller and more timely consultation with the Office of Legal Adviser on issues of similar import.[9]

A second function of legal justification is to assist in legitimating the action taken to relevant publics at home and abroad. A country that asserted at birth 'a decent respect for the opinions of mankind' should be the last to disparage that exercise. The Declaration of Independence is, in fact, a typical example of the kind of *ex post* justification we are here discussing. Despite its recitals, nobody would argue that it states the 'reasons', in a causal sense, that lay behind the decision for independence. The Declaration is an effort to justify that decision in terms of a set of generally applicable principles. It was one aspect of a campaign to mobilize the support, at home and abroad, without which the decision, no matter how resonant, could not have been carried out.

For these purposes, international law justification has two special features. First, the norms of international law comprise a special set of 'generally accepted principles' to which appeal can usually be made without arguing separately the validity of the principles. This is a convenience that was unavailable to the men who asserted the inalienability of the right to life, liberty, and the pursuit of happiness. That principle derived its legitimacy—its power to compel adherence—not from law, but from the philosophy of the Enlightenment. It remains true that legal norms are not the only basis upon which national decision can be and is justified, even when justification is sought in terms of 'neutral principles'. Nevertheless, international law does provide a fairly rich and complex body of norms and procedures, validated as to general acceptability and prescriptive content independently of the particular case to which they are applied. Even Gerberding, whose uncomplimentary remarks were quoted above,[10] concedes that

---

N.Y.U. L. Rev. 628 (1970); Stevenson, 'The International Law Issues—Administration Position', id. at 648.

[9] 'Rogers Memo on Legal Issues Reported', *N.Y. Times*, 24 June 1970, p. 3, col. 3. The *N.Y. Times* quoted Secretary Rogers as stating in the memo, 'Finally, public, Congressional and international support also depends on a prompt and convincing demonstration of the legality of our actions; we cannot afford to wait until action is taken to start preparing our case.'

[10] P. 41 *supra*.

. . . presumably most governments—especially the genuinely uncommitted ones—were in search of some balance of equities around which they could build their own position. Legal norms express or imply values that are common to most men and most governments most of the time, at least in the abstract. . . .[11]

Secondly, justification is not simply an appeal to some vague 'world public opinion', whose reactions affect the course of events only remotely and indirectly, if at all. The international legal system is almost exclusively a horizontal system, rather than a hierarchical one. The sanctions of the system, such as they are, consist not in the imposition of penalties by specialized organs empowered for the purpose, and to that extent hierarchically superior to the actor, but in the responses of other governments, independent entities on the same formal plane as the actor. In such a system, the role of justification is more than the mobilization of support or acquiescence from these other independent actors. Failure to justify in terms of international law warrants and legitimizes *disapproval* and negative responses from the other governments participating directly in the process.[12]

ii

What evidence is there that the justification for the quarantine at international law did in fact contribute to legitimizing United States action? Can we identify any effect on the attitudes of other states or important groups by way of mobilizing support or mitigating opposition? For the purposes of this question we may take the decision to refer the issue to the O.A.S. and its approval of the quarantine under the Rio Treaty as the essence of the justification, deferring for the moment a more detailed analysis.

The initial response of the Soviet Union to the President's speech was to put the legality of the quarantine in issue. Its announcement of 23 October accused the United States of 'piratical acts' and 'unheard of breaches of international law'.[13] Most United States officials were relieved by this response, considering the alternatives that had been anticipated, and regarded

---

[11] Gerberding, n. 1 *supra*, at 197.

[12] Henkins, *How Nations Behave* 46–52 (1968).

[13] 'Text of Soviet Statement Challenging the U.S. Naval Quarantine of Cuba', *N.Y. Times*, 24 Oct. 1962, p. 20, col. 2; and see Topping, 'Moscow Replies', *N.Y. Times*, 24 Oct. 1962, p. 1, col. 8.

it as evidence that the Soviets had been taken by surprise and were unsure of what course to follow.[14]

But, if leaders in Washington were prepared to disparage the Soviet legal attack, they took a good deal of comfort from the unanimous action of the O.A.S. the same day authorizing the quarantine. Accounts of the crisis are agreed in general about the impact of the O.A.S. action. Robert Kennedy says that 'our position around the world was greatly strengthened when the Organization of American States unanimously supported the recommendation for a quarantine'.[15] And in his summary he concludes 'Their willingness to follow the leadership of the United States was a heavy and unexpected blow to Khrushchev. It had a major psychological and practical effect on the Russians . . .'[16]

Elie Abel, writing rather closer in time to the events, describes the initial impact as follows:

In New York, Adlai Stevenson was delivering his opening speech in the Security Council when Harlan Cleveland, then Assistant Secretary of State for International Organization Affairs, gave him a note about the unanimous O.A.S. vote. Elated at the outcome, Stevenson promptly read the O.A.S. resolution into the record of the Security Council. There is reason to think that Moscow was staggered by the show of inter-American solidarity. . . .[17]

The *New York Times* summary of 3 November, generally confirms the later accounts.

The unanimity of the [O.A.S.] council, together with the solid support of the NATO allies for the blockade decision, is believed by officials to have surprised the Soviet Union and to have accounted for much of her diplomatic confusion during the week.[18]

But what of Robert Kennedy's parting shot to Leonard Meeker at the Friday morning meeting to the effect that the significance of the O.A.S. reference was political, not legal?[19] From what has already been said, we should recognize that these categories

[14] Hilsman at 211; Sorensen at 709; Abel at 127-8.
[15] Kennedy at 51; Sorensen at 706.
[16] Id. at 121.
[17] Abel at 131.
[18] *N.Y. Times*, 'Cuban Crisis: A Step-by-Step Preview', 3 Nov. 1962, p. 7, col. 3.
[19] See p. 16 *supra*, and n. 34, p. 15 *supra*.

are far from watertight. International law is not unique in this respect. All law, especially public law, is political in the sense that it embodies political values and judgments. Constitutional law is political in the sense that it is often principally concerned with which institutions are empowered to make these judgments. International law has an additional political dimension in that its sanction and enforcement mechanisms, such as they are, are almost exclusively political.[20] The opportunities and costs of legal justification are precisely the political responses of the states, institutions, and publics involved.

The opinion testimony quoted above is subject to some discount. Yet other kinds of evidence are likely to be tenuous at best. One or two minor, almost trivial incidents provide indirect support for the conclusion that the legal justification had importance for some significant audiences.

The decision to go to the O.A.S. posed a problem for the drafting of the President's speech, which was to be delivered before the O.A.S. was called into session. If the justification of O.A.S. approval was to be available, the President could not take final action before the O.A.S. considered the matter. Yet there was a possibility that O.A.S. might not approve. And everyone felt the need to convince the Soviets and Cubans, as well as the rest of the world—including the O.A.S. members themselves—of the firmness of the United States purpose. The dilemma and its resolution are noted by Sorensen in describing his review of the speech draft with the President:

Would he [the President] institute the blockade without the O.A.S. approval? Yes, if we could not get it, because our national security was directly involved. But hoping to obtain O.A.S. endorsement, he deliberately obscured the question in the speech. . . .[21]

The language of the speech seems sufficiently forthright:

To halt this offensive build-up, a strict quarantine on all offensive military equipment under shipment to Cuba is being initiated. All ships of any kind bound for Cuba from whatever nation or port will, if found to contain cargoes of offensive weapons, be turned back. . . .[22]

---

[20] See Chayes, 'A Common Lawyer Looks at International Law', 78 Harv. L. Rev. 1396, 1410 (1965).

[21] Sorensen at 699.

[22] [1962] *Public Papers of the Presidents, John F. Kennedy* 807 (1962).

Contrast it however, with the words of the quarantine proclamation, issued twenty-four hours later, after the O.A.S. had acted:

NOW, THEREFORE, I, JOHN F. KENNEDY, President of the United States of America . . . do hereby proclaim that *the forces under my command are ordered,* beginning at 2 : 00 P.M. Greenwich time October 24, 1962, *to interdict,* subject to the instructions herein contained, *the delivery of offensive weapons and associated material of Cuba.* [Emphasis added] [23]

Immediately after the President's speech there was a press briefing for perhaps 150 reporters in the State Department auditorium, conducted by Under Secretary George Ball and myself.[24] Within ten minutes the reporters had located the ambiguity Sorensen refers to. They spent the better part of the next hour trying to get it resolved: 'What would we do if the O.A.S. refused to approve the quarantine?' The question was asked and re-asked in every conceivable form. For the officials on the receiving end, the point of the game was to evade the question as best they could, which they managed, if somewhat lamely, to do. (In consequence, this particular briefing produced very little news.) Reporters, in the conventional wisdom, are practical, hard-bitten men. Yet they concentrated on the issues raised by the legal justification of the action almost to the exclusion of the other aspects of the President's decision, most of which seemed of far greater practical consequence at the time.

There was a second incident of a similar kind. The Legal Adviser's Memorandum, reprinted in this volume as Appendix III, is the contemporaneous official exposition of the government's legal position. It was prepared over the night and morning of 22–23 October, and was made available after the Organ of Consultation had acted. For a variety of reasons, primarily related to the haste with which the document had to be drafted, it was decided not to release it officially. It was to be distributed in unclassified form as 'guidance' to officers in discussing the legal issues. The instructions permitted the full text to be made available on request to any interlocutor, including members of the press. The extent of the demand for this document was a complete surprise to me. The pleas from our diplomatic missions

[23] Id. at 810. This Proclamation recited the O.A.S. resolution as one of its sources of authority.
[24] Hilsman at 207; Sorensen at 704; Abel at 125–6.

for an exposition of the legal basis for the United States action were so insistent and continuous that soon after the O.A.S. action and the quarantine proclamation on the evening of 23 October, the wires were cleared and the memorandum was transmitted in full to all posts. An edition of 500 copies was made up and forwarded to the United States mission at the U.N., where they were promptly distributed in response to requests. Another 500 had to be supplied. In a week of compelling high-level prose, the anonymous and unauthenticated memorandum became something of a best-seller.

It would be wrong to make too much of these two incidents. Perhaps they are no more than chit-chat reminiscence of great events from one severely limited professional perspective. But they seem to me to show in particularly concrete form that 'mere' justification carries greater practical importance for the success or failure of great decisions than is commonly supposed by the analysts.

The men most closely involved thought so. Sorensen describes how, after the greatest danger had passed on Sunday 28 October, the members of the Executive Committee waited for the President, speculating on the 'what ifs'—the things that might have changed the outcome if they had been different. The second entry on an eight-item list is 'what would have happened . . . if the O.A.S. and other Allies had not supported us'.[25]

iii

Did the justification justify? From what is said above, we know that the question cannot be translated 'Was the United States position "right" as a matter of law?' On that score, it should be said at once that the official position has not been fully accepted by many, perhaps most, of the scholars who have addressed the issue, even those who supported the validity of the United States action.[26]

---

[25] Sorensen at 716; and see Kennedy at 120–1.

[26] See, e.g., Wright, 'The Cuban Quarantine', 57 Am. J. Int'l L. 546 (1963); Campbell, 'The Cuban Crisis and the UN Charter: An Analysis of the United States Position', 16 Stan. L. Rev. 160 (1963); Partan, 'The Cuban Quarantine: Some Implications for Self-Defense', [1963] Duke L. J. 696; and Standard, 'The United States Quarantine of Cuba and the Rule of Law', 49 ABA J. 744 (1963).

The relevant question, we have said, is whether there was a professionally serious and responsible effort to deal with the legal issues. The United States position is embodied in the Memorandum on the Legal basis for the Quarantine of Cuba and a number of contemporaneous official speeches, in large part of my own authorship.[27] It is not wholly comfortable, therefore, to undertake an answer to the question here.

The matter is further complicated because the memorandum, although written as an advocate's brief, is categorical in tone, more in the manner of a judicial opinion than an academic analysis. Like the judicial opinion, it was designed to develop the main affirmative line of reasoning supporting the result, without dealing with hypothetical cases not before the authors. Like the judicial counterpart, it labours under the requirement of not anticipating the future and taking positions that may be hard to disavow in later, unforeseen circumstances.

Despite these apologies and reservations, it has seemed to me that in order to validate the functional role of the legal arguments as a justification of the action, some sense of their substantive complexity and professional texture is necessary. Moreover, there may be some value in stating the position a bit more fully than was possible at the time.

The Organization of American States

The memorandum concentrates on the textual sources of authority for O.A.S. action in Articles 6 and 8 of the Rio Treaty. There is comparatively little difficulty in establishing that the missile crisis could reasonably be characterized as a 'fact or situation that might endanger the peace of America'[28] or that the quarantine was within the available sanctions enumerated in Article 8. The major legal issue was the relationship of this authority under the Rio Treaty to the provisions of the U.N.

[27] See N.Y. Bar Assoc., *Third Hammarskjold Forum: The Inter-American Security System and the Cuban Crisis* 31–56 (1964); Chayes, 'Law and the Quarantine of Cuba', 41 Foreign Affairs 550 (1963); Remarks of Abram Chayes before the Harvard Law School Class of 1952 on 3 Nov. 1962, 47 Dep't of State Bull. 763 (1962): and Meeker, 'Defensive Quarantine and the Law', 57 Am. J. Int'l L. 515 (1963).

[28] Inter-American Treaty of Reciprocal Assistance (hereinafter 'Rio Treaty'), 2 Sept. 1947, 62 Stat. 1681 (1948), T.I.A.S. No. 1838, 21 U.N.T.S. 77 (effective 3 Dec. 1948), Art. 6; and see Appendix III, pp. 141–3.

Charter. This accords with the judgment of most scholars.[29] If there had been no United Nations, it seems fairly clear that the powers of the Organ of Consultation under the Rio Treaty were ample to support the action taken as against a member of the organization. There are, however, three issues of some difficulty apart from U.N. questions. The general outlines of a response on all three were at least adumbrated at the time and can be stated here somewhat more fully.

First, the basic reason for preferring collective to unilateral decision in crisis cases is the likelihood of a more balanced and many-sided, less biased appraisal of the situation and the remedies called for. It is an application on the international plane of the principle of checks and balances. The memorandum touches on this point. '[Regional] organizations', it says, 'have close contact with the problems within their regions and thus can exercise considered and informed judgment in dealing with these problems. The Organization of American States is a prime example of this. The political process by which it must operate ensures that action will only be taken after careful analysis.'[30] The same point is made somewhat more explicitly in a later article in *Foreign Affairs*, '. . . decisions are made by political processes involving checks and balances and giving assurance that the outcome will reflect considered judgment and broad consensus.'[31]

This reasoning fails, however, if the decision, though in form collective, is in reality simply the expression of the will of a dominant power. O.A.S. action is vulnerable to such criticism because of the extreme disproportion of power, measured on any scale, between the United States and the other members, individually and collectively.[32] The Soviets, as was to be expected, charged that the O.A.S. had acted as the puppet of the United States.[33] In response to this line of argument, the Office of Legal Adviser said:

[29] See n. 26 *supra*.
[30] Appendix III at 145.
[31] Chayes, 'Law and the Quarantine of Cuba', n. 27 *supra*, at 554. See Gerberding, n. 1 *supra*, at 207–8, commenting on this process: 'The implication of this position is that *any* regional organization can, providing its political processes "give some assurances that the decision will not be rashly taken", sanction the use of force "to deal with a threat to peace".' For a response to this objection, see pp. 53–5 *infra*.
[32] Franck, 'Who Killed Article 2(4)? or: Changing Norms Governing the Use of Force by States', 64 Am. J. Int'l L. 809, 822–6, 832–3 (1970).
[33] See U.N. SCOR, 1022nd Meeting 33 (1962).

The significance of the political processes in the Organization [of American States] is attested by the fact that, despite the disproportion of power between the United States and its neighbors to the south, it was not until the danger was clear and present that the necessary majority could be mustered to sanction use of armed force. But when the time came, the vote was unanimous.[34]

The reference is to the indifferent record of the United States in mobilizing the O.A.S. on Cold War and Cuban issues. At Caracas in 1954,[35] at San José in 1960,[36] and at Punta del Este in 1962,[37] despite the expenditure of considerable political capital, the objectives of the United States had been blunted in the arena of parliamentary diplomacy.[38] Even though in every case the necessary majorities were mustered for some kind of anti-Communist or anti-Cuban pronouncement, on no occasion was the United States able to obtain unanimous support, even for a compromise resolution.[39] The hold-outs included some of the

[34] Chayes, Remarks 47 Dep't of State Bull. at 764–5 (1962).

[35] Pan American Union, The International Conferences of American States, Supp. II 1942–1954, 30 Dep't of State Bull. 420 (1954).

[36] Declaration of San José, Costa Rica, 29 Aug. 1960, Final Act of the Seventh Meeting of Consultation of Ministers of Foreign Affairs, OEO/Ser. F/II.7, 43 Dep't of State Bull. 407–8 (1960).

[37] Res. VI of Eighth Meeting of Consultation of Ministers of Foreign Affairs, 31 Jan. 1962, OEA/Ser. F/II.8, Doc. 68; II Pan American Union, Inter-American Treaty of Reciprocal Assistance, Applications 75–6 (1964), 46 Dep't of State Bull. 281 (1962).

[38] American efforts to gain support for its positions at these conferences had met with only partial success. At the Caracas Conference, the delegates adopted a Declaration of Solidarity for the Preservation of the Political Integrity of the American States against International Communist Intervention, but the text was not as strong as the United States had proposed. Pan American Union, n. 35 *supra*, at 423–5. At the 1960 San José Conference, the United States was unable to secure a formal denunciation of Communism or the Castro regime. Declaration of San José, n. 6 *supra*, at 4–5, 43 Dep't of State Bull. 407–8. Finally, at the Punta del Este Conference in 1962, the United States barely succeeded in having Cuba excluded from participation in the Organ of Consultation even though all recognized the alliance between Castro and the Soviet Union. Res. VI of Eighth Meeting, n. 37 *supra*, at 17–19, 46 Dep't of State Bull. 281; and see Res. of the Council of Delegates, 26 Apr. 1961, [1961] O.A.S. Secy. Gen. Ann. Rep. 12.

[39] At the Caracas Conference, the Declaration was adopted by a vote of 17–1, with two abstentions. Pan American Union, n. 35 *supra*, at 420. At the Punta del Este Conference in 1962, only 14 of the 21 members of the O.A.S.—the minimum two-thirds requirement—voted to support an American resolution concerning Cuba's exclusion. Res. VI of Eighth Meeting, n. 37 *supra*, at 17–19, 46 Dep't of State Bull. 281. At that Conference, the Foreign Ministers

strongest and most important Latin American countries.[40] In the month preceding the crisis, the idea of going to the O.A.S. for authorization of reconnaissance overflights of Cuba had been abandoned, in part because of the fear that the necessary support would not be forthcoming.[41]

The unamimity of the response on the quarantine was surprising even to the United States officials closest to the organization. Assistant Secretary Edward Martin, at the 19 October meeting, guessed that seventeen votes was perhaps the maximum that could be safely expected.[42] There is no doubt that the members of the Organ of Consultation were under heavy pressure to endorse the United States proposal.[43] The President's speech of Monday night and the personal appearance of the Secretary of State at the O.A.S. meeting on Tuesday[44] were designed to structure the situation so as to maximize the sense of urgency and gravity. But there is no reason to doubt the conclusion of contemporary observers that the unanimity reflected, as well, an independent perception of danger among the Latin American states.[45] Concrete evidence of independence of judgment is seen in the reservations and abstentions of some members on portions of the resolution. Mexico, Brazil, Bolivia, and Uruguay ab-

---

voted to suspend trade with Cuba '. . . in arms and implements of any kind'. But again, the support was less than unanimous. The resolution was adopted by a vote of 16–1 with four abstentions. Id., Res. VIII, II Applications at 77–8, 46 Dep't of State Bull. 282 (1962).

[40] Those opposing or witholding support for the American positions at these Conferences have frequently been the larger and more influential Latin American Countries. At Caracas, Mexico and Argentina abstained. At Punta del Estes, Brazil and Mexico abstained on both resolutions, and Argentina joined them on the exclusion resolution. 46 Dep't of State Bull. 281 n. 10, 282 n. 12 (1962).

[41] See pp. 20–1 *supra*.

[42] See pp. 16, 34 *supra*; n. 34, p. 15 *supra*. Abel says that Martin first thought the chances of securing O.A.S. approval of the American position to be 1 in 4, and later on believed that, 'with luck', the necessary 14 votes might be won. Abel at 104, 129. Both of these estimates seem unduly pessimistic. See n. 27, p. 34 *supra*.

[43] According to Meeker, Martin thought it desirable to approach all the Latin American heads of state before the O.A.S. meeting, and this necessitated delaying the President's speech by a day. See n. 27, p. 34 *supra*. See also Sorensen at 696–7.

[44] See O.A.S. Official Records, Minutes of Special Meeting, 23 Oct. 1962, OEA/Ser. G/II/C-a-462, at 4–9, 47 Dep't of State Bull. 720–2 (1962).

[45] See, e.g., Abel at 130.

stained on the second clause of the second paragraph authorizing further action in addition to the quarantine if that should prove ineffective.[46] Mexico expressed an understanding that support for the American resolution did not expand the constitutional authority of the executives within O.A.S. countries to dispatch armed forces outside their countries without the consent of their respective legislatures.[47]

All in all, the record shows that, although the Organ of Consultation, like every parliamentary assembly, was not an assemblage of equals, it was neither supine nor a rubber stamp for a United States initiative.

Second, the United States argument had to be more than a blanket charter for collective use of force by a multi-national grouping. What was to distinguish the O.A.S. action on the quarantine from action by, let us say, the Arab League against Israel or the O.A.U. against South Africa? From action by the Warsaw Pact against Hungary (or, subsequently, Czechoslovakia)?[48]

The two examples are not identical. The first case—Arab League *v.* Israel—can be distinguished on the ground that Cuba was a member of the O.A.S., which Israel is not of the Arab League. Despite efforts to limit its participation, Cuba had not withdrawn from the organization or repudiated its adherence to the relevant treaties. On the contrary, it maintained that the efforts to deprive it of participation were illegal.[49] As a party to the O.A.S. Charter and the Rio Treaty, Cuba had assented to the powers and procedures of the organization. Its case was therefore very different from that of a non-member of a regional organization, against whom the organization had moved. Implicit in this argument is the conclusion that *vis-à-vis* non-members the regional organization is limited to collective self-defence against armed attack within the meaning of Article 51 of the U.N. Charter.

Gerberding says the '. . . argument that Cuba in effect assented to the blockade because she was technically still a member

[46] O.A.S. Official Records, Minutes of Special Meeting, 23 Oct. 1962, OEA/Ser. G/II/C-a-463 21, 26.

[47] Id. at 18, 26.

[48] See Franck, n. 32 *supra*; Gerberding, n. 1 *supra*, at 183–4, 207–8.

[49] See, e.g., Letter from Representative of Cuba to President of Security Council, 22 Feb. 1962, 17 U.N. SCOR, Supp. Jan.–Mar. 1962, at 82, U.N. Doc. S/5080 (1962).

of a regional organization that sanctioned it is so bizarre as to
require no refutation'.[50] But the point is not that Cuba assented
to the blockade. The point is that she agreed to the processes that
approved the blockade and so was bound by the result of those
processes, just as the loser in an election or a lawsuit is bound,
even though he thinks the result is wrong. The Treaty authorized
the Organ of Consultation to determine whether a particular
'fact or situation . . . might endanger the peace of America', and
if so 'to agree on . . . the measures which should be taken . . .
for the maintenance of the peace and security of the Continent'.[51]
These are political judgments, not legal questions. The legal
significance of the Treaty is that it empowered the Organ of
Consultation to make these judgments authoritatively. Cuba
could not legally complain simply because she did not like the
result.

This United States argument is more vulnerable to the point
that Cuba was no longer a member of the O.A.S. in the full sense
of the term, having been 'excluded from participation in its
organs' by the resolution of Punta del Este earlier in the year.[52]
The counter to this contention has already been discussed above.[53]

For the second case—the Warsaw Pact *v.* Hungary, or for that
matter NATO *v.* Greece—the distinction turns on the scope and
character of the agreement among the parties. The defence
alliances in Eastern and Western Europe are collective self-
defence arrangements pure and simple, having their basis in
Article 51 of the U.N. Charter. By contrast, the O.A.S. is also
a regional arrangement under Chapter VIII, with broad authority for the adjustment of disputes among members and the
enforcement of its decisions. Professor Thomas Franck, in a recent
article, points to this potential distinction:

The discussions at the San Francisco Conference do, of course, clearly
support the proposition that the regional groupings then in being regarded themselves, *ipso facto*, as beneficiaries of the new provisions in
Article 51 which authorize the use of force in collective self-defense without prior United Nations approval. But does it follow, conversely, that
any organization set up primarily to take advantage of the right to act
in collective self-defense under Article 51, thereby also qualifies *ipso*

---

[50] Gerberding, n. 1 *supra*, at 207.
[51] Rio Treaty, n. 28 *supra*.
[52] See n. 37 *supra*.
[53] See p. 20 *supra*; and Appendix II at 137.

facto as a regional organization, entitled to maintain 'peace and security' among its members under Article 52 and 53?[54]

Franck notes that the United States answered this question in the negative in the context of the action by Warsaw Pact members against Czechoslovakia in the summer of 1968.[55] But this was no novel formulation. It has been a consistent United States position with respect to 'pure' collective self-defence organizations, including NATO. In 1956, for example, when asked whether NATO 'might assume jurisdiction' in a case like the then rapidly deteriorating Cyprus situation, Secretary Dulles answered:

You see, at the present time NATO is not set up as a regional association under the United Nations Charter. It is set up as a collective self-defense association.

. . . Now so far, as I say, NATO has not been organized as a regional association, nor has it any policy or jurisdiction to deal with disputes as between the members. One of the matters which will doubtless be considered [at forthcoming Atlantic Council meetings] in evaluating the desirable evolutionary steps to be taken at this time would be that question of whether or not to make it more of a regional association with the responsibility to settle differences between its members.[56]

The Legal Adviser's Memorandum is premissed on this distinction. It is the point of the elaborate demonstration that the action of the O.A.S. falls within the powers expressly granted by the Treaty. No such demonstration could be made with respect to the North Atlantic Treaty or the Warsaw Pact.[57]

[54] Franck, n. 32 *supra*, at 827.
[55] Ibid.
[56] Dep't of State Bull. 925–6 (1956).
[57] Professor Franck's article suggests that qualification as a regional organization with jurisdiction to settle internal disputes and to apply sanctions including the use of force, depends on some objectively ascertainable level of regional integration. The level is to be determined in the first instance, he argues, by reference to the degree of integration achieved by the prototype regional organization, the O.A.S., at the time of San Francisco. The Legal Adviser's Memorandum is at odds with that view. Chapter VIII does not establish a norm, against which regional organizations are to be measured willy-nilly, but a facility, which regional organizations, whatever their degree of integration, are free to employ if they choose. The choice is to be registered in the constitutive documents of the organizations. Professor Franck's review of charters of existing regional groups shows that they are very chary on just this matter of granting to the organization express dispute-settlement authority backed by sanctions. One might be willing to imply some such authority from

Third, the threat of force implicit in the quarantine operated not directly against Cuba but against the Soviet Union and other third parties with ships in the quarantine area. These states had not assented to the jurisdiction of the O.A.S. Thus, for example, Quincy Wright was willing to grant that the resolution 'may apply in respect to Cuba, because it had consented by the O.A.S. and Rio Treaties to the use of sanctioning methods against itself if recommended by the Consultative Organ of the Organization of American States'. But, he insisted, the resolution 'could apply only to the American states and not to the Soviet Union'.[58]

There is an anomaly in Wright's position. The effects of an invasion or air strike would have been confined primarily to Cuba. Thus, on his view, these measures would have been within the power of the O.A.S. to authorize. But the lesser action of blockade was not, because its effects were spatially more diffuse. We should be unwilling to accept an argument that would deny to regional organizations engaged in internal-dispute settlement the more moderate end of the range of response.

Moreover, whatever the measures taken, their impact could be limited to Cuba only in a superficial sense. Third parties would necessarily be affected. The Soviets had large deployments on the island; other countries had other interests. To adopt Wright's view would be to disable a regional organization from acting under provisions like Articles 6 and 8 of the Rio Treaty. For no regional dispute—or none but the smallest—is hermetically sealed inside the confines of the region, without ramifications on the larger international scene. If regional organizations are to function effectively as peace-keeping agencies in such disputes, their actions will necessarily impact more or less significantly upon states outside the region.

This can be tolerated so long as the U.N. has jurisdiction to assert the broader international interest when the nature and extent of the impacts outside the region seem to warrant it. Considerable latitude may be granted to regional efforts, if the U.N.

---

an extended course of conduct in which an organization exercised such juris-diction with the assent of all, or from policy statements and communiqués falling short of formal international agreement. But given the universal re-luctance of states to accept third-party settlement mechanisms, one should not be quick to assume assent to the jurisdiction of a regional organization without a pretty explicit textual basis.

[58] Wright, 'The Cuban Quarantine', [1963] Proc. Am. Soc. Int'l L., 9–10.

remains free to assess the balance of intra-regional and global considerations, giving such weight as it thinks appropriate to the ability of the regional organization to deal with a dispute having major local aspects—and to decide whether, and to what extent, it wishes to supersede or displace the action of the regional organization.

The existence of a U.N. concurrent and supervisory jurisdiction was conceded in the Legal Adviser's Memorandum,[59] and developed somewhat more fully in several contemporaneous official statements:

Regional organizations, of course, remain subject to check even where, as in this case, they employ agreed procedures and processes. They are subordinate to the U.N. by the terms of the Charter and in the case of the O.A.S., by the terms of relevant inter-American treaties themselves. Like an individual state, it can be called to account for its action in the appropriate agency of the parent organization.[60]

By this route, the legal defence of the United States position returns us again to the central question of the relation between regional action and the universal organization.

The United Nations

The legal relation of regional action to the U.N. has two distinct aspects. The first is in the operation of Article 53 of the Charter, which provides that '. . . no enforcement action shall be taken . . . by regional agencies without the authorization of the Security Council'.[61] Secondly, there is the general supervening authority of the U.N., implicit in the hierarchical relation between the two international organizations.

The Legal Adviser's Memorandum would drastically limit the scope of Article 53. The technical argument is set in the context of a broader conception of the constitutional history of the U.N. Granting that the original understanding at San Francisco was to give the Security Council far-reaching positive authority over action by regional organizations, this was part of an integrated concept of the Security Council as an active and effective peacekeeping organ. That concept was not vindicated in the activities of the organization over the then decade and a half of its life.

---

[59] Appendix III at 141.
[60] N.Y. Bar Assoc., n. 27 *supra*, at 54.
[61] U.N. Charter, Art. 53 (1).

The affirmative powers of the Council, the most extensive that had been granted until that time to any international political body, were, in the event, semi-paralysed by the operation of the veto.[62] If the affirmative peacekeeping powers of the Council were neutralized, why should it be permitted to play dog-in-the-manger and keep others out of the field?

There was U.N. practice in support of the argument that an impasse in the Security Council should not be permitted to thwart other organizational peacekeeping efforts. Almost from the beginning, the Secretary-General on his own authority, and often in the face of a divided Council, intervened in important disputes.[63] The furthest reach of assertion of peacekeeping authority in the face of a deadlocked Security Council was the creation of the U.N. Emergency Force in 1956 to keep the peace in the Middle East.[64] The force was set up by the Secretary-General under the authority of General Assembly resolutions,[65]

---

[62] This does not necessarily imply a one-sided criticism of the U.S.S.R. Once the veto became a functioning part of the system, in the political battles of the Cold War it was a matter of primarily tactical significance that its exercise was mostly on the part of the Soviet Union. That reflected only the political balance in the Council, not necessarily the location of right and justice. When western interests were infringed by the line-up in the Council, as at Suez, western permanent members exercised their veto; see 11 U.N. SCOR, 749th Meeting 31 (1956); and 11 U.N. SCOR, 750th Meeting 5 (1956); and there is no doubt that the United States would do so in a similar political situation where its own interests were engaged; see 25 U.N. SCOR, 1534th Meeting (1970), 62 Dep't of State Bull. 501 (1970). That it had not done so by 1962 was a reflection of its political dominance in the Council, not necessarily of a fundamentally different attitude towards the institution.

There was some concern at the San Francisco conferences that the veto might paralyse the Security Council. To remedy this, some states sought an explicit definition of aggression in Article 2(4), which would automatically trigger appropriate sanctions without having to depend on the vote of the Security Council. See U.N.C.I.O., *Documents*, vol. 3 at 585 (1945) (amendment proposed by Bolivia); Russell, *A History of the United Nations Charter* 669–775 (1958). But these efforts were overridden.

[63] See generally Schwebel, *The Secretary-General of the United Nations* (1952); and see Gordenker, *The UN Secretary General and the Maintenance of Peace* 172–81 (1967); Boan, *The Leadership Role of the Secretary General in Times of International Crisis* 115ff. (1965) (U.Va. Ph.D. dissertation).

[64] G.A. Res. 997 and 998, 1st Emergency Spec. Sess., U.N. GAOR, Supp. 1, at 2, U.N. Doc. A/3354 (1956).

[65] G.A. Res. 1000 and 1001, 1st Emergency Spec. Sess., U.N. GAOR, Supp. 1 at 2, 3, U. N. Doc. A/3354 (1956); and see, generally, Committee on the Study of Legal Problems of the U.N., 'The Establishment of the United Nations Emergency Force', [1957] Proc. Am. Soc. Int'l L. 206.

after England and France had vetoed Security Council action.[66]

One might argue that if peace-keeping authority is to be extended beyond the Security Council, it should at least be confined to organs of the U.N. itself. On the other hand, Chapter VIII of the Charter provides at least an equally persuasive basis for the argument that regional organizations, properly empowered, should also be available for peacekeeping, assuming the break-up of the Security Council monopoly. For the United States, the choice between these two views was not a question of first impression. In Security Council debates on O.A.S. action in regard to Guatemala, the Dominican Republic, and even Cuba itself, the United States had staked out its position that the O.A.S. had concurrent if not primary jurisdiction to deal with disputes in the hemisphere, and even power to impose sanctions, at least until the Security Council acted to assert its own powers under the Charter.[67] The only remaining issue was whether the present case, the first involving use of force by a regional organization, could be squared technically with the language of Article 53.

Article 53 contains two operative concepts, neither of which is self-defining: 'enforcement action' and 'authorization'. The Legal Adviser's Memorandum focuses on the first of these, arguing for the narrowest of readings.[68] It maintains that if the action by a regional organization is recommendatory rather than mandatory in character it cannot be enforcement action. Since the O.A.S. resolution was only a recommendation—it was so drafted in part for this very purpose—it escaped the strictures of Article 53. Earlier O.A.S. sanctioning activity had been mandatory in form, and in each of those cases, the United States had also argued that 'enforcement action' was not involved.[69] The memorandum distinguishes these cases as not involving the use

[66] U.N. SCOR, 749th Meeting, 31 (1956); U.N. SCOR, 750th Meeting, 5 (1956).

[67] For the United States position in the Guatemala case, see 9 U.N. SCOR, 675th Meeting, 29–35 (1954); on the Dominican Republic situation see 15 U.N. SCOR, 893rd Meeting, 8–9 (1960); on the Cuban situations, see 15 U.N. SCOR, 874th Meeting, 27–8 (1960). See also Franck, n. 32 *supra*, at 822–6.

[68] Appendix III at 146-8.

[69] See 15 U.N. SCOR, 893rd Meeting, 8–9 (1960); 17 U.N. SCOR, 991st Meeting, 18–19 (1962); and, in general, II Chayes, Ehrlich and Lowenfeld, *International Legal Process* 1077–92 (1968); n. 67 *supra*.

of force. The residual scope of the concept of 'enforcement action' is thereby further narrowed to include only those actions by a regional organization that are at the same time mandatory and involve the use of force.

The opinion of the World Court in the Certain Expenses case[70] is cited in support of this proposition. In that case, the Court upheld the power of the General Assembly to establish the U.N. Emergency Force in the Middle East. To do so, the opinion had to deal with the requirement of Article 11(2) that questions affecting peace and security 'on which action is necessary shall be referred to the Security Council by the General Assembly'. The Court upheld the Assembly's power by defining the terms 'action' and 'enforcement action' to include only mandatory decisions, as opposed to recommendations.[71]

The opinion points out, however, that the General Assembly resolution establishing the Emergency Force was recommendatory not only as to the states contributing troops, but also as to Egypt on whose territory the force was to be deployed. In the absence of a mandatory decision of the Security Council under Chapter VII, the validity of the deployment of the force depended on Egypt's consent.[72] By parallel reasoning, Cuba's consent was necessary if the O.A.S. action on the quarantine was to escape the category of 'enforcement action'. That consent was present only if, with Quincy Wright, one is prepared to derive it from Cuba's adherence to the Rio Treaty.[73] The comfort to be found in the specific language used by the I.C.J. may

---

[70] *Certain Expenses of the United Nations*, [1962] I.C.J. 151.

[71] 'The word "action" must mean such action as is solely within the province of the Security Council. It cannot refer to recommendations which the Security Council might make, as for instance under Article 38, because the General Assembly under Article 11 has a comparable power. The "action" which is solely within the province of the Security Council is that which is indicated by the title of Chapter VII of the Charter, namely "Action with respect to threats to the peace, breaches of the peace, and acts of aggression". If the word "action" in Article 11, paragraph 2, were interpreted to mean that the General Assembly could make recommendations only of a general character affecting peace and security in the abstract, and not in relation to specific case, the paragraph would not have provided that the General Assembly may make recommendations on questions brought before it by States or by the Security Council. Accordingly, the last sentence of Article II, paragraph 2, has no application where the necessary action is not enforcement action.' Id. at 165.

[72] Id. at 170.

[73] Wright, n. 58 *supra*, at 9–10.

therefore be somewhat thin. But on any view, the Court's opinion was important in vindicating the growth of international peacekeeping capability outside the Security Council, and, indeed, in the teeth of vetoes in the Council.

A final difficulty with the treatment of 'enforcement action' in the memorandum was that under Article 20 of the Rio Treaty, 'no state shall be required to use force without its consent'. Given this language, could O.A.S. action ever involve mandatory use of force? If not, the result would be that the O.A.S. could never conduct 'enforcement action' as defined in the Legal Adviser's Memorandum.

Each of these objections could be rebutted, but the position was unwieldy enough to cause a shift in official exposition towards a second approach. Rather than narrowing the scope of 'enforcement action', it sought to expand the concept of 'authorization' under Article 53. Very probably the Framers at San Francisco would have said, if they had thought about it, that the word denoted prior and express approval by the Council. But the idea of 'authorization' is broader than that in most legal systems.[74] Prior U.N. practice lent support to some extension. In particular, when the O.A.S. imposed economic sanctions on the Dominican government of Trujillo in 1960, the Soviets themselves seemed to take the position that approval *ex post* by the Council would satisfy the requirement of authorization in Article 53.[75] To cover the case of the quarantine, the concept had to be stretched further to include failure of the Security Council to disapprove the regional action, at least, where as in the Cuba case, a member 'introduced a resolution of disapproval, but by general consent it was not brought to a vote'.[76]

United States official statements took these extra steps. It is clear at this point, however, that the argument is struggling with the unworkability of Article 53, at least in situations where the interests of a permanent member of the Council are heavily involved. If the burden is on the regional organization to secure affirmative endorsement by the Council it must fail; if the burden is on the opponent of regional action to secure explicit disapproval

---

[74] See, e.g. Restatement (Second) of Agency §§7, 8, 26, 27, 43 (1957); Ryan, *An Introduction to the Civil Law* 72–6 (1962).

[75] The Soviet position is reflected in the remarks of Ambassador Kuznetsov in 15 U.N. SCOR, 893rd Meeting, 2–5 (1960).

[76] Chayes, n. 27 *supra*, at 556.

it must fail. The United States takes the second horn of this
dilemma. It avoids reading Article 53 out of the Charter entirely
only by attributing significance to various kinds of expressions
and actions of the Council short of the formal adoption of a
resolution.

This would be an unsatisfactory outcome if Article 53 were the
only vehicle by which the U.N. could assert its interest or policy
in the matter. The United States went on, however, to recognize
a general hegemony of the U.N., a kind of reserve power implicit
in its character as a universal organization to which all regional
bodies must ultimately be subordinate. If the concession is to
avoid reviving the Article 53 dilemma in another form, it must
acknowledge the possibility that U.N. hegemony could be expressed not alone by the Security Council, but also by action of the
General Assembly. This was done, if somewhat elliptically, by
statements that the O.A.S. 'can be called to account for its action
in an appropriate agency of the more encompassing organization'.[77]

iv

The foregoing argument had enough soft spots to induce careful consideration of the alternatives. The only other justification
that seemed potentially available[78] was the one Mr. Katzenbach
put forward at the 19 October meeting, the principle of self-
defence.[79] The self-defence argument comes in two technically
different versions, each stressing a different aspect of the language
of Article 51:

[77] E.g. N.Y. Bar Assoc., n. 27 supra, at 54. The theory received a certain
corroboration in the 1965 Dominican affair. The O.A.S. constituted an Inter-
American peacekeeping force (consisting largely of United States troops already
on the island). Tenth Meeting of Consultation, Resolution of 6 May 1965,
OEA/Ser. F/II.10 Doc. 39, Rev. 2, 52 Dep't of State Bull. 862 (1965). The
Security Council was unwilling to condemn the O.A.S. action and unable, by
virtue of a threatened Soviet veto, to approve it. The Security Council then
authorized the Secretary-General to send a representative to the Dominican
Republic. 20 U.N. SCOR, 1208th Meeting 2–3 (1965). The O.A.S. with some
grumbling, acquiesced. Although nobody bothered at the time to sort out the
legal categories, what emerged in practice looks suspiciously like concurrent
jurisdiction concurrently exercised. See generally, Chayes et al., n. 69 supra, at
1174–217.
[78] But see Henkin, How Nations Behave 238–9 (1968).
[79] p. 15 supra; see n. 34, p. 15 supra.

Nothing in the present Charter shall impair the inherent right of individual or collective self-defense if an armed attack occurs. . . .[80]

The first construes 'armed attack' to cover a broad range of threats, thus permitting anticipatory self-defence even though use of force could not be said to be imminent. The second version argues that 'the inherent right' of self-defence extended beyond cases of armed attack, and this broader right was preserved without impairment by the article. In practice, these two approaches, put forward concurrently by the same proponents, tend to merge.[81]

The self-defence argument in either form was never officially espoused in the Cuban affair.[82] On the contrary, it was repeatedly and consciously rejected. For example, the penultimate draft of the President's speech had a reference to Article 51 just before the words 'We no longer live in a world where only the actual firing of weapons represents a sufficient challenge to a nation's security to constitute maximum peril.'[83] In the Legal Adviser's Office, it was thought that the citation of Article 51 in combination with those words would amount to a full-scale adoption of the doctrine of anticipatory self-defence. In a phonecall to Theodore Sorensen, I urged that the reference should be deleted: it was inconsistent with the effort to obtain O.A.S. endorsement and would be unnecessary if that effort were

[80] U.N. Charter, Art. 51.

[81] See, e.g., McDougal, 'The Soviet–Cuban Quarantine and Self-Defense', 57 Am. J. Int'l L. 597 (1963); Fenwick, 'The Quarantine Against Cuba: Legal or Illegal?', 57 Am. J. Int'l L. 588 (1963); MacChesney, 'Some Comments on the "Quarantine" of Cuba', 57 Am. J. Int'l L. 592 (1963); Christol and Davis, 'Maritime Quarantine: The Naval Interdiction of Offensive Weapons and Associated Material to Cuba', 57 Am. J. Int'l L. 525, 533–6 (1963); Alford, 'The Cuba Quarantine of 1962: An Inquiry into Paradox and Persuasion', 4 Va. J. Int'l L. 35, 42–6 (1964); Mallison, 'Limited Naval Blockade or Quarantine Interdiction: National and Collective Defense Claims Valid under International Law', 31 G.W.L. Rev. 335 (1962).

[82] Christol and Davis, n. 81 *supra*, at 534–5 review evidence they argue supports the view that the United States made a claim of self-defence under Article 51, and Mallison, n. 81 *supra*, at 353, is even more emphatic. Sorensen, at 699, says the President deleted a specific reference to Article 51, 'but carefully chose his words for anyone citing that article'. It is true that until the O.A.S. acted there remained some possibility that Article 51 might be the only real defence open, and in any case no one wished expressly to disavow it. But that is a different matter from claiming the benefit of the Article.

[83] [1962] *Public Papers of the Presidents, John F. Kennedy* 807.

successful.[84] Sorensen agreed to put the matter to the President, who according to Sorensen's book, deleted the reference.[85]

Furthermore all of the O.A.S. documentation refers expressly to Article 6 of the Rio Treaty, dealing with a situation 'which is not an armed attack', rather than Article 3, dealing with cases of armed attack. The distinction was first made in the passage of the President's speech announcing that the Organ of Consultation was being convoked[86] and was maintained right on until the text of the final resolution.[87] The point was underscored in the Memorandum on the Legal Basis for the Quarantine of Cuba.[88]

Finally, during the week after the President's speech, a campaign was mounted within the Department to secure the official adoption of a self-defence rationale. It was argued that the weaknesses in the justification based on O.A.S. authorization were beginning to emerge. The government's law officers, it was said, were no different from any other lawyer arguing his client's case before a tribunal. They had the right and even the duty to put forward all plausible arguments that could be made in good faith in defence of the action. The issue was finally resolved by the Secretary of State personally, not, to be sure, on the merits, but on the ground that, in a matter falling within the bureaucratic responsibility of the Legal Adviser, his views should prevail.

Why this elaborate effort to eschew Article 51 and self-defence as a justification? It can hardly be said that no reasonable man could have characterized the situation as one falling with Article 51. A large fraction of United States international-law scholarship has followed precisely that road.[89] The characterization would have been challenged. But so were many of the crucial points in the official justification actually put forward. Neither approach could have been authoritatively invalidated—or validated for that matter—for there was no tribunal or agency empowered to

---

[84] In one sense, the refusal to characterize the missile emplacement as an armed attack can be seen as an aspect of the general effort to communicate to the Soviets the sense that the United States was acting with restraint and caution, and did not see the situation as an occasion for all-out response.

[85] Sorensen at 699–700; see n. 82 *supra*.

[86] [1962] *Public Papers of the Presidents, John F. Kennedy* 808.

[87] Resolution of the Organ of Consultation, OEO/Ser. G/II/c-a-463 at 25 (1962); see also Interdiction of the Delivery of Offensive Weapons to Cuba, Proclamation No. 3504, 23 Oct. 1962, 27 Fed. Reg. 10401 (1963).

[88] Appendix III, at 141.

[89] See n. 81 *supra*.

give a determinative answer. Why not, then, make the self-defence argument?

Intra-office discussions at the time emphasized that it would set a bad precedent if the United States were to rely on a self-defence theory.[90] Nobody believed that the United States characterization of its action would be given a kind of binding force in a later case. Still less would we have argued that if the Soviet Union should find itself similarly situated it would act with greater restraint because the United States had refused to invoke Article 51 in the Cuban case. Nevertheless, the normative atmosphere in which states act, though tenuous and impalpable perhaps, is affected by the earlier actions of others and their accompanying statements of what they take the governing law to be. An official United States position endorsing a latitudinarian construction of 'armed attack' could not help but weaken those normative checks.[91] To this extent there was something in the idea that a claim of self-defence would set a dangerous precedent.

In retrospect, however, I think the central difficulty with the Article 51 argument was that it seemed to trivialize the whole effort at legal justification. No doubt the phrase 'armed attack' must be construed broadly enough to permit some anticipatory response. But it is a very different matter to expand it to include threatening deployments or demonstrations that do not have imminent attack as their purpose or probable outcome. To accept that reading is to make the occasion for forceful response essentially a question for unilateral national decision that would not only be formally unreviewable, but not subject to intelligent criticism, either. There is simply no standard against which this decision could be judged. Whenever a nation believed that interests, which in the heat and pressure of a crisis it is prepared to characterize as vital, were threatened, its use of force in response would become permissible.

This, it seems to me, reduces to Mr. Acheson's position: 'law simply does not deal with such questions of ultimate power—power that comes close to the sources of sovereignty'.[92] It may be that Mr. Acheson is right—either in the sense that the law *ought* not to reach such situations or in the empiric sense that it *does* not as a matter of practice. But, right or wrong, it is certainly

---

[90] See Abel at 115; cf. Gerberding, n. 1 *supra*, at 183–4.
[91] See generally Franck, n. 32 *supra*.
[92] Acheson, 57 Proc. Am. Soc. Int'l L. 13, 14 (1963).

not a *legal* justification. To dress the Acheson view up in the language of the Charter does justice neither to Mr. Acheson nor to the international legal system.

In this sense, I believe an Article 51 defence would have signalled that the United States did not take the legal issues involved very seriously, that in its view the situation was to be governed by national discretion not international law. Some may regard that conclusion as inherently reprehensible; others as refreshingly candid. In either case, it would have meant that values other than law were being chiefly relied on as justification for action. If legitimation by law was needed or wanted, the Article 51 argument could not really carry the burden.

v

The justification, it turns out in the end, was more than merely a justification. It operated in part as a constraint as well. In order to have available the legal argument based on O.A.S. endorsement it was necessary to submit the action to the O.A.S. for consideration before the final orders were given. So the decision was not just a decision for a quarantine. It was a decision, in addition, to submit the matter in the first instance to the O.A.S. At a minimum, therefore, the felt need for justification affected the pattern of execution in a decisive way, although it must be added that the political values of O.A.S. endorsement, if indeed these can be separated from the legal consequences, operated to the same effect.[93]

The reference to the O.A.S. was integral to the quarantine decision itself. It was not something 'worked out *after* the basic decision was made'.[94] The final evidence of this is its inclusion in the President's speech as part of the action programme he announced.[95] But the same close relation between O.A.S. endorsement and the quarantine choice was evident throughout the planning stage. Robert Kennedy's summary of the scenarios for the two alternatives to be presented to the President is instructive to this point:

. . . For the group that advocated the blockade, it was an outline of the legal basis for our action, an agenda for a meeting of the Organization

[93] Kennedy at 51; Sorensen at 706; Abel at 131; Hilsman at 211.
[94] Gerberding, n. 1 *supra*, at 201.
[95] [1962] *Public Papers of the Presidents, John F. Kennedy* 808.

of American States, recommendations for the role of the United Nations, the military procedures for stopping ships, and, finally, the circumstances under which military force might be used. For the group that advocated immediate military action, it was an outline of the areas to be attacked, a defense of our position in the United Nations, suggestions as to how to obtain support from Latin American countries, and a proposed communication to Khrushchev to convince him of the inadvisability of moving militarily against us in the Caribbean, Berlin, or elsewhere in the world.[96]

The first element of the quarantine scenario is 'an outline of the legal basis for our action' followed immediately by a developed 'agenda for a meeting of the Organization of American States'. Only after these steps as well as the United Nations aspects had been outlined, did the scenario turn to the operational problems of initiating and conducting the blockade on the high seas. The air-strike scenario, on the other hand, although it deals with the problem of obtaining 'support from Latin American countries', does not implicate the O.A.S. as such, at least in Kennedy's recollection.

It may be said, however, that once the quarantine was decided upon, there was no real constraint involved in the step of prior submission to the O.A.S., since that course did not entail any surrender of freedom of action, or even any serious additional risks. It could hardly have seemed a significant possibility that the thirteen Latin American votes needed for O.A.S. action would not be forthcoming.[97]

Robert Kennedy, at least, was not so confident. Moreover, if Sorensen is clear, after the fact, that the quarantine would have gone forward even without O.A.S. support, Kennedy, before, was more reserved. In the 19 October meeting, he was sensitive to the consequences in the event, however remote, of an O.A.S. turndown. He argued that the President would be placed in an impossible position if the United States went to the O.A.S. and then failed to get the necessary votes, or if there were a delay.[98] The consequences would have been less serious, but by no means negligible, if the vote of approval had been by a bare majority, particularly one made up of the smaller and presumably more pliable members of the organization. If there was no risk of out-

---

[96] Kennedy at 45.   [97] But cf. n. 42 *supra*.

[98] N. 34, p. 15 *supra*; Sorensen at 706 states that the President 'had been concerned about getting the necessary two-thirds vote . . .'.

right disapproval there was a risk that the debate would reveal deep-seated political division in the hemisphere.

The time element stressed by the Attorney General was also important. In retrospect, the effect of the quarantine in stretching out the crisis and affording time for deliberation in move and counter-move has seemed to be one of its most important assets.[99] But at the time, there was desperate urgency to get the United States action under way before the whole matter leaked to press and public, and, even more important, before the missiles became operational. This, it was thought, would alter the situation decisively.[100] To predict that the O.A.S. would ultimately sustain the United States initiative may have been comparatively easy. To give assurance that this would happen on a time-scale consistent with the felt requirements was much more difficult. As it was, one of the main reasons for putting off the President's speech from Sunday to Monday—a delay that nearly resulted in premature disclosure—was Assistant Secretary Martin's view that it would be virtually impossible to get to the Latin American heads of state on Sunday.[101] It cannot be said, therefore, that the reference to the O.A.S. was a gesture in the direction of legalism, adopted at the stage of execution, carrying no risks for the basic policy chosen.

In the final analysis, the problem of justification influenced not only the execution, but the choice of the quarantine as well. Quite apart from whether they thought the United States *ought* to obey the law, the men involved knew it would be desirable to be able to offer a strong legal justification for their action, though this desideratum did not carry the same weight for everyone. The lawyers were agreed that prior reference to the O.A.S. and approval by that body would immeasurably strengthen the justification for whatever action was taken. But the quarantine was the only course that permitted prior reference to the O.A.S. One of the considerations listed as inclining the President himself in this direction is that 'It could be carried out within the framework of the Organization of American States and the Rio Treaty.'[102] Thus the need or desire that United States action be capable of public justification in law became a factor operating differentially to favour the quarantine.

[99] See e.g., Kennedy at 111.   [100] See p. 25, n. 9, *supra*.
[101] See n. 43 *supra*.
[102] Schlesinger, *A Thousand Days* 805–6 (1965).

V

LAW AS ORGANIZATION:
THE O.A.S. AND THE U.N.

i

THE growth of international organizations is the most important development in the international legal system in the post-war period. Until 1940, international organizations were few, and United States attitudes towards them, as opposed to judicial-type approaches to adjustment of international conflict, were symbolized in the rejection of the League of Nations by the Senate in 1920.[1] In the years after 1945, there was an organization explosion on the international scene, in which the United States, perhaps by way of expiation, played the leading role. At latest count the United States was a member of nearly 100 international organizations.[2] Of these, the O.A.S. and the U.N. are distinctive as political organizations having more or less plenary jurisdiction to consider international issues within their respective geographic spheres. From the perspective of a decade later, it is remarkable how large an arc of the decision-makers' horizon in the Cuban missile crisis was occupied by these two organizations.

International organizations are at once product and source of international law. They are created by agreement among the members, and agreement among states is the most widely acknowledged and unchallengeable basis of international law.[3] Indeed the International Court of Justice with an imperial sweep that would have done credit to Chief Justice Marshall, has characterized every question of interpretation of the U.N. Charter as 'essentially a judicial task, namely, the interpretation of a treaty provision'.[4]

That is hyperbole. The treaties that create international

---

[1] 59 Cong. Rec. 4600 (1920).

[2] Chayes, Ehrlich, and Lowenfeld, *International Legal Process* x–xi (1968); and see Henkin, *How Nations Behave* 21, and n. 4, p. 274 (1968).

[3] See, e.g., Statute of the International Court of Justice, Art. 38(1) (a), 26 June 1945, 59 Stat. 1031 (1945), J.R. No. 993 (effective 24 Oct 1945).

[4] *Certain Expenses of the United Nations*, [1962] I.C.J. 151, 155 (1962).

organizations are treaties of a very special kind. Most are called—officially or unofficially—Charters. The taxonomy signifies that they are essentially constitutive documents. Like most constitutions, they are not so much concerned with defining rules of conduct—substantive norms—as they are with establishing the jurisdiction of the organization and allocating to its various parts their power and authority to act.

Because of their formal, multilateral, and considerably public structure, the international organizations tend to generate 'law' and 'legal' issues, a consequence that even lawyers may not regard as an unmixed blessing. For good or ill, issues tend to get deflected from the merits, and to be discussed in jurisdictional terms. Organizations 'act' mainly by resolution. So again, issues tend to get converted into exercises in draftmanship or into debates over the meaning of previously adopted resolutions. Plenary organs tend to take on the character of legislative assemblies; relations with secretariats manifest many of the characteristic features of executive/legislative relations in more fully sovereign political bodies.

An international organization is not a sovereign, 'not', as the World Court said, '. . . a State . . . still less, . . . a "super state" . . .'[5] But it *is* a political body and it does act. Not in the manner of a political entity with a full complement of attributes of sovereignty, and not very often in ways that fulfil popular expectations and demands for action. But every international organization acts, and it acts to some degree independently of the governments that are its members. This is so even when, as is usually the case, its powers are recommendatory or are otherwise qualified.

The organization acts independently of governments because although the delegates who sit in it are representatives of their governments, they are not the same as the governments they represent. The delegate is subject to instructions. These may be very general in the case of smaller and newer nations, whose foreign offices are also less developed. In a country like the United States or the U.S.S.R., the instructions are normally elaborately detailed, designed to leave little scope for the representative's discretion. But the ambassador, who will ordinarily be more sensitive to the institutional pressures of the organization to which

[5] *Reparations for Injuries Suffered in the Services of the United Nations*, [1949] I.C.J. 174, 179 (1949).

he is attached than are his principals in the capital, usually has a good deal to say in the formulation of his own instructions, especially when as has often been the case with the United States representatives in the U.N., he has independent political stature. Moreover, even detailed instructions raise all the familiar problems of insuring that the delegate complies. And in the end, the man on the spot must move and speak in reaction to the fast-moving (for diplomacy) flow of floor debate.[6] Finally, even in moments of intensest crisis, the ambassador's instructions will come not from the whole government he represents, but at most the executive leadership of that government. In the United States and many other countries, the result is that the instructions reflect a different amalgam of national and international interests and considerations from what would be the case if legislative concurrence were required, as at the time when the Charter of the organization was ratified.

A recommendation has force because it represents a mandate, a political consensus. As such it is a fact with which any country operating within the ambit of that recommendation must deal. Moreover, the action even if recommendatory, translates the vague and rather flexible consensus that underlies it into the concrete text of a specific resolution. Subsequent argument and debate is focused and channelled, issues are defined in terms of the words of the resolution adopted. The resolution is not 'binding' and compliance may not be forthcoming. But it is there, a fact of political life that must be taken into the calculus by a state even in the very process of violating its provisions.

All of these characteristics of international organizations deriving from their discrete legal entity were in evidence in the Cuban missile crisis. The most significant consequence of the institutional setting, however, was that the very existence of the organizations altered the array of requirements and opportunities that faced American decision-makers.

ii

The decisive factor impelling the United States to seek approval of its policy in the O.A.S. may have been not so much the sense of legal obligation or the prospect of legal legitimation, but simply

[6] Consider, e.g., the problem of the Bolivian representative to the O.A.S. during the missile-crisis debate, pp. 73–4 *infra*.

that it was there. It would have been, in fact, a practical impossibility for the United States to take the kind of action proposed against Cuba without some form of review in the O.A.S. Through two administrations the organization had been a central element of the United States policy against Communism in the western hemisphere, and specifically against Cuba. At every stage of its confrontation with the Castro government, the United States sought the support and co-operation of the O.A.S.[7] That support was not always forthcoming in full measure, but nevertheless, the United States spent lavishly of political capital to secure the backing of the countries with whom it presumably shared the threat and the danger. The O.A.S. was the vehicle that had been used to express a common western-hemisphere appraisal, common concern, common response. Even if the issue of O.A.S. endorsement had been all politics, as Robert Kennedy said,[8] the legal incarnation of the organization was what created the political problem, or at least defined the terms in which it had to be faced. To have ignored the O.A.S. when the danger so long forewarned finally materialized in palpable form, would have made a mockery of the talk and commitments of a decade.

Again, we must be on guard against the anthropomorphic fallacy. Perhaps the single chessplayer could have afforded to sacrifice the O.A.S. piece. But not the men actually playing this game. They had made statements, engaged their word, formed associations with counterparts in the O.A.S.

For the President, not only his Cuban policy but the Alliance for Progress, which had for him even broader implications, was rooted in the organization.[9] For the Secretary of State, the Latin American Foreign Ministers were colleagues whom he knew and had worked with personally. Only two weeks earlier at a meeting in Washington he had been rallying them to the danger inherent in Cuban developments and arguing the need for collective response.[10] If the President and Secretary were personally engaged, for Edwin M. Martin, Assistant Secretary for Latin

---

[7] See pp. 51–2 *supra*.

[8] See p. 16 *supra* and n. 34, p. 15 *supra*.

[9] See generally, Schlesinger, *A Thousand Days*, chaps. VII, VIII, XXIX (1965).

[10] See p. 21 *supra*; *N.Y. Times*, 3 Oct. 1962, p. 1, col. 4. Secretary Rusk personally led the delegation to Punta del Este in Jan. 1962. See Schlesinger, n. 9 *supra*, at 780ff.

America, the organization was his daily preoccupation. He was continuously concerned in its affairs; had spent countless hours with its representatives and would have to face them many times again in the future; had devoted much of his thought and energy to giving reality, or the appearance of reality, to the O.A.S. as a vehicle for collective action in the hemisphere. And again, the bureaucratic fact was that the position of his office in the State Department and its involvement in the crisis would be in part a function of how heavily and centrally the O.A.S. was involved. Martin, in fact, was the only Assistant Secretary of State in the Executive Committee; his presence at the table at this stage was undoubtedly attributable in part to the potential O.A.S. involvement.[11]

It is not inconceivable that the Executive Committee could have been brought to cut through this intricate web of personal and official engagement. But the brief sketch above suggests some of the political and psychological hurdles on that path. I believe that ultimately, the O.A.S. would have been involved, even if the decision had been for air strike or invasion. In that case the organization would have been asked to endorse a United States *fait accompli*, at some sacrifice of all the interests—legal, political, personal, bureaucratic, and tactical—that were served by a prior reference to the O.A.S. Some support for this view is found in the Dominican episode three years later, when the Johnson administration did act without the support of an O.A.S. resolution, in the first instance, but was impelled within a few days to seek one.[12]

If the existence of the O.A.S. as a legal organization could be seen to present a political problem for United States policy, its formal structures and procedures were an important asset in mobilizing hemispheric support. They made it possible to formulate the issue of support in terms of a specific text, having operational significance, that had to be voted up or down by each participating state. The issue was drawn in public, under the glare of television lights, with a tight deadline. The pressure generated by the situation is revealed in the action of the Bolivian

---

[11] See Sorensen at 706. Martin was also the operating officer with responsibility for Cuban affairs. His counterpart, the Assistant Secretary for European Affairs, however, was not among those present. Paul Nitze also carried the rank of Assistant Secretary, but in the Department of Defense.

[12] Materials are collected in Chayes, Ehrlich, and Lowenfeld, n. 2 *supra*, at 1150–1233.

representative. Bolivia was at that time boycotting the O.A.S. Council on an unrelated issue. Although special telephone connections were established for communications with Latin American capitals, a satisfactory telephonic circuit was never opened up with the La Paz. Finally, the Bolivian delegate voted for the resolution on his own responsibility.[13]

The organizational structure provided little room for qualifying the stark 'yes' or 'no' response. Brazil and one or two other delegations raised questions about the scope of the resolution in authorizing forceful action, presumably including an invasion of Cuba, in addition to the quarantine.[14] They were able, procedurally, to secure a sentence-by-sentence vote, and to abstain on the objectionable language.[15] Nevertheless, in the end the resolution had to be voted up or down as a whole, and these states voted with the others.

To the extent that the support of Latin American countries was a factor of political importance for United States policy, the O.A.S. provided a wellnigh indispensable vehicle for getting it. Formidable difficulties and wide variations in response would have resulted if it had been necessary to round up this support in the nineteen Latin American capitals. The parallel effort to rally NATO for the United States initiative is illustrative.[16] NATO, as a defence organization, was, it would seem, much more consequential than the O.A.S. The European countries are more powerful on any scale on which international power is measured. The North Atlantic alliance was implicated by the action taken. The quarantine line was within the NATO area as defined in Articles 5 and 6 of the North Atlantic Treaty. An attack on a United States ship enforcing the quarantine would have been 'an armed attack . . . on the vessels . . . in this area of [one] of the Parties', an event expressly calling for action by the alliance under the Treaty.[17] The most likely Soviet responses were

---

[13] Abel at 130–1; Hilsman at 211.

[14] O.A.S. Official Records, Minutes of Special Meeting, 23 Oct. 1962, OEA/Ser. G/II/C-a-463 at 21–2, 26 (1962).

[15] Id. at 25.

[16] See Abel at 128–9; Sorensen at 705–6.

[17] North Atlantic Treaty, Art. 6, 4 Apr. 1949, 63 Stat. 2241 (1949), 34 U.N.T.S. 243 (effective 24 Aug. 1949). The Article defines the treaty area to include 'the North Atlantic area north of the Tropic of Cancer'. Although Cuba itself is south of the Tropic of Cancer, the principal quarantine line, 500 miles north, was well within the defined area.

thought to be a blockade of Berlin or an attack on the missiles in Turkey, both at the heart of NATO concern.[18]

The NATO Council, however, is not a forum for expressing the political will of the North Atlantic Alliance in the same way the Organ of Consultation is for the O.A.S. We have already commented that this makes a difference in what NATO is legally empowered to do.[19] Here we see an institutional difference in what it can practically be used to do. NATO, as an organization, is designed for planning, preparing, and conducting the defence of Western Europe, not for taking political action. The only corporate action taken by NATO during the missile crisis was a resolution recommending support of the United States position in the Security Council.[20] Since it was apparent that, in the initial stages, there would not be anything to vote on in the Security Council, this action had little significance.

The three principal European allies of the United States— Britain, France, and West Germany—were approached individually on a bilateral basis. This was mainly because of their importance, but also in part because there was no institutional forum available. Their responses illustrate some of the disadvantages of such an approach, as opposed to the more structured and formal setting of an international organization. United States Ambassador in London, David Bruce, supported by a specially dispatched photo-interpreter, told Prime Minister Macmillan on Monday. Mr. Acheson, as the President's personal emissary, visited the heads of state of France and Germany the same day.[21] All three governments, as a result, publicly endorsed the United States position, and there is no doubt that these prompt expressions of support had significant political impact.[22] Yet in each case the announcement was general. It did not commit any government to any particular action. The language of the statements differed considerably, and conveyed, as they were intended to do, differences in the depth and quality of support.[23]

---

[18] See Abel at 86–7; Sorensen at 685, 689.

[19] See pp. 54–5, *supra*.

[20] See 47 Dep't of State Bull. 831 (1962).

[21] See Kennedy at 51–2; Abel at 109–10; see Sorensen at 705; Hilsman at 211–12.

[22] See, e.g., Kennedy at 121.

[23] The *N.Y. Times* reported 'The British Government pledged firm support tonight for United States policy toward Cuba. The Earl of Home, the Foreign Secretary, accused the Soviet Union of "duplicity" and of "deliberately"

These differences may have been simply a matter of nuance, but the contrast between the British statement and the French suggests that they were deeper than that. And, in the last analysis, the statements were not votes. A vote on a resolution has a finality about it. It is a fact and its significance is evidenced by a text that others also have read, interpreted, and adhered to. Later action can qualify it in some ways, but it remains on the record as the formal and considered expression of position on a sharply drawn question. A statement of support is informal and much more open-ended. Its content is only made manifest by subsequent actions as concrete occasions for manifesting support appear. In the case of both England and Germany, there was reason for concern whether in the event the support would live up to the statements and whether it would be durable.[24]

I do not mean to exaggerate the difference in the response of European and Latin American allies. Robert Kennedy,[25] as well as other observers,[26] have bracketed O.A.S. and NATO in describing the impact of the political support of the United States allies on the Soviet Union. This discussion is meant primarily to illustrate the differences in diplomatic and political technique that are introduced into the process of mobilizing support when an international institution is in the picture. The analysis sug-

---

threatening the United States, the Caribbean area, and Latin America. A strong Foreign Office statement declared that the Soviet Union had been "guilty of deception" in Cuba and of opening "a new area of instability". The statement described as a "provocative action" the Soviet Union's building of nuclear missile bases in Cuba.' Middleton, 'Home Denounces Soviet', *N.Y. Times*, 24 Oct. 1962, p. 1, col. 3. *The Times* described the French Government's reaction as follows: 'President de Gaulle, who received Mr. Acheson's report late yesterday afternoon, considered himself to have been "informed but not consulted". In consequence, there was no formal French statement of solidarity to match the one issued in London. Instead, the closest thing to an official French position was a statement by Pierre Baradue, spokesman for the French Foreign Ministry. He spoke in Brussels in the name of the foreign ministers of the six countries of the European Economic Community, or Common Market, who studied the Cuban situation there today. He said that the ministers "expressed comprehension of the United States position in the Cuban affair and of the measures taken by the Government of Washington". He added that the ministers "are naturally preoccupied with the possible developments of that affair".' Doty, 'Lack of Talks Annoys Paris', *N.Y. Times*, 24 Oct. 1962, p. 1, col. 4.

[24] See p. 97 *infra*.
[25] Kennedy at 121–2.
[26] E.g., Sorensen at 705–6; Abel at 131.

gests, however, that the differences are not alone at the level of technique, but involve the substantive character of the response as well.

iii

The United Nations also was 'there'. The General Assembly was in the early stages of its annual session when the crisis began. Gromyko's presence in the United States for the opening of the session provided the occasion for him to visit the President on Thursday 18 October.[27] The Security Council, in compliance with the mandate of the Charter, was 'so organized as to be able to function continuously'.[28] The coincidence of the rotation schedule placed the Russian delegate, Ambassador Zorin, in the chair that month. It seemed inevitable that the United States action would be brought before the Council promptly after it was announced, and that it might ultimately be debated in the Assembly as well. The problem for United States planners was not whether the U.N. would be seized of the issues, but how.

The first question was whether the United States would appear in answer to charges of the U.S.S.R., or whether it would itself take the initiative in presenting the questions to the Security Council. For both lawyers and politicians, there was little to commend the role of defendant. If, then, the United States was to move affirmatively to bring the crisis to the U.N., it remained to shape the strategy and form of the initiative.

The Security Council was the indicated forum, at least to begin with. Under the Charter that organ has 'primary responsibility for the maintenance of international peace and security'.[29] With eleven members, debate and action could be kept under better control, even with Zorin in the chair, than in the more diffuse and unwieldy General Assembly. The United States could count on support from its allies among the permanent members, Britain, France, and Nationalist China, as well as from Venezuela, Chile, and Ireland, who were then sitting on the Council.[30] The seven votes insured a working majority on all issues and would be decisive on procedural questions.

[27] See Sorensen at 689–91; Abel at 74–5; and Kennedy at 39–40.
[28] U.N. Charter, Art. 28(1).
[29] Id., Art. 24(1).
[30] 17 U.N. SCOR 1022d Meeting, 1 (1962).

In what form would the approach to the Security Council be cast? A moment ago I used the familiar terms of the adversary system—plaintiff and defendant. There is undoubtedly a strong current of expectation, in the United States anyway, that the United Nations *should* be a tribunal to sit in judgment upon the parties to international disputes, deciding who is right and who is wrong, and fashioning remedial action accordingly. A closer acquaintance with the organization soon reveals that these expectations are misplaced. Except in very special cases, the Council has not exercised anything like an adjudicative role in disputes, especially when the parties are the United States and U.S.S.R. The Council does not like to 'take sides'. The reluctance is based partly on political grounds. The members of Council cohabit the same world with the disputants, and have myriad other interests and relations with them, apart from the particular dispute or even the U.N. Votes on Security Council questions affect these other interests, and no one wishes to offend if it can be avoided.

There is a further basis for the unwillingness to take sides, more closely related to the functional needs of the Council as such. The Council is and usually conceives itself as a political body, fostering political solutions to political problems. Such solutions are not readily developed in terms of 'right' and 'wrong' but in terms of accommodation of the interests at stake. The process involved is mediatory or even legislative, rather than adjudicative. Taking sides hinders that process.

The characteristic response of the United Nations in major crises had been some kind of standstill resolution, an effort to stop the shooting and slow down the momentum of the crisis to give time for cooler heads to prevail.[31] From the point of view of United States planners in October 1962, a standstill, which was a highly likely Security Council response, would be quite unsatisfactory. As they saw it, a standstill would prevent further Soviet seaborne deliveries and it would stop the quarantine. But it would not get the missiles out of Cuba, nor even halt the work that was bringing them daily closer to operational readiness.

---

[31] See, e.g., the action of the United Nations in the Suez crisis of 1956, G.A. Res. 997 and 998, 1st Emergency Spec. Sess. (Doc. A/3354) (1956); in the Cyprus crisis, 19 U.N. SCOR Supp. Jan.–Mar. 1964, 102–3 (Doc. S/5575) 1964); and in the Dominican Republic crisis of 1965, 20 U.N. SCOR, 1204th Meeting (Doc. S/6346) (1965).

On the contrary, it was feared that a standstill resolution would permit Soviet construction crews to work ahead at their own tempo while the debate ground on in the Council. Moreover, during this time it would be much more difficult for the United States to escalate in any way that would intensify the pressures on the U.S.S.R. and Cuba.

It followed that one of the central objectives of United States strategy in the United Nations was to forestall a call for a standstill. The veto in the Security Council was not a complete answer to that problem. Often the evolution of debate and parliamentary diplomacy puts a Permanent Member in a position where the veto becomes an unappealing prospect. At a minimum, there would be a significant political cost if the United States were to be forced to use its veto for the first time against Security Council action in this crisis, especially against an apparently even-handed standstill resolution.

Moreover, the Security Council was not the only possible forum. The General Assembly, under the Uniting for Peace Resolution[32] and related procedures formulated with United States leadership, could take a hand in the matter, and in that body there was no veto. The Secretary-General, on his own, has a certain authority. His powers are based on the barest of Charter references,[33] but they had been assiduously cultivated by the holders of the office, again with the strong encouragement of the United States.[34] By 1962, the office disposed of powers that began to look something like an independent executive authority.

Finally, it was by no means clear that adverse pressure in the U.N. would limit itself to a call for a standstill. Nobody could predict the reaction to the President's speech. It was pretty certain

---

[32] G.A. Res. 377 (V) (1950); and see pp. 30–1 *supra*.

[33] U.N. Charter, Art. 97, 98, 99. The Secretary General is designated as 'the chief administrative officer of the Organization,' he is required to make 'an annual report to the General Assembly on the work of the Organization,' and 'he may bring to the attention of the Security Council any matter which in his opinion may threaten the maintenance of international peace and security'.

[34] Notable manifestations of this support were the United States leadership in the extension of Trygve Lie's term as Secretary-General over Soviet opposition based on Lie's conduct in the Korean action. See Chayes, Ehrlich, and Lowenfeld, n. 2 *supra*, at 161–2 for a brief summary, and the Kennedy administration's fight against Khrushchev's 'troika' proposal in 1962, a proposal originating in Dag Hammarskjold's strong executive leadership of the Congo operation. See, e.g., id. at 165.

that once the crisis was made public, the world would know that it was closer to a nuclear showdown than ever before. That perception might very well translate itself, whether from disapproval or from fear, into a U.N. demand that the United States not only stand still, but stand down.

Given the tactical problems of controlling U.N. reaction and preventing a standstill resolution or worse, an obvious gambit was to go into the United Nations with a position that showed a willingness to settle the dispute on a 'reasonable' basis—that was, in the jargon of the State Department, 'forthcoming'. This was the setting against which the details and documentation of the United States recourse to the U.N. were developed.

A good deal of controversy has developed over the preparation of the U.N. position, and in particular about the role of Ambassador Stevenson in it. Elie Abel's account is as follows:

Stevenson had approved the blockade decision, insisting that O.A.S. approval was vital. On Saturday afternoon he started thinking aloud about further diplomatic moves. The President, he urged, should consider offering to withdraw from the Guantanamo naval base as part of a plan to demilitarize, neutralize and guarantee the territorial integrity of Cuba. Stevenson held that Guantanamo, in any event, was of little value. He also forecast grave difficulties concerning the Jupiter bases in Turkey. People would certainly ask why it was right for the United States to have bases in Turkey, but wrong for the Russians to have bases in Cuba. The President, he said, should consider offering to remove the Jupiters in exchange for the removal of Russian missiles from Cuba. Perhaps U.N. inspection teams could be set up to inspect all foreign bases, Russian as well as American, to guard against a surprise attack while the dismantling was being carried out.

Kennedy addressed himself directly to Stevenson's proposals, rejecting both. The United States, he said, simply could not at this stage consider giving up Guantanamo. As for the Jupiters, the President had his own doubts about their continued value and was willing to consider removing them in the right circumstances. But this was not the time for concessions that could wreck the Western alliance; seeming to confirm the suspicion Charles de Gaulle had planted that the United States would sacrifice the interest of its allies to protect its own security. Dillon, Lovett and McCone sharply attacked Stevenson, but the U.N. Ambassador stood his ground. This was the exchange that later led to published charges that 'Adlai wanted a Munich'. In fairness to Stevenson, Paul Nitze submits that as Ambassador to the United Nations, 'Adlai had to be the one who looked at this proposition from the U.N. standpoint, the standpoint of simple equities and the hazards of war.' Dean Rusk's impression is that Stevenson was not in fact advocating an American withdrawal from Guantanamo or from Turkey. He was trying to suggest what kinds of demands might be raised if, as many others also expected, the Russians dragged their feet after agreeing to remove the missiles from Cuba and thus involved the United States in a long wearying negotiation.

Stevenson's own recollection was that he argued the United States ought to be willing to pay some price for the neutralization of Cuba if that meant getting the Russians out, along with their missiles. The bitter aftertaste of that Saturday afternoon in the Oval Room stayed with him until his death.[35]

I cannot corroborate or contradict this account from personal observation. However, I very much doubt that the thrust of United States strategy in the U.N. was finally decided at that meeting. The State Department group working on U.N. aspects of the crisis chaired by Ambassador Stevenson met next morning with Secretary Rusk. A proposal for a Security Council resolution embodying significant mutual concessions was put forward by Ambassador Stevenson and apparently seconded by the Secretary. The discussion considered a trade of Turkish for Cuban missiles as well as other similar moves either as alternatives or in addition to such a trade. Among these possibilities were a nuclear-free zone in Latin America or the Caribbean, perhaps covering parts of United States territory, with some inspection of United States facilities, and a general prohibition of forward deployments of strategic missiles on both sides. Without necessarily committing himself to such an approach, the Secretary encouraged the group to pursue it.

No doubt the individuals in the group differed in their appraisals of the wisdom of such proposals on their merits. But a dominant consideration was the tactical situation that would be faced in the Security Council beginning Tuesday morning. The feeling was widespread among the members of the Executive Committee that the Turkish missiles would have to be given up in the end, as the price of settlement. The same view was expressed almost unanimously at a somewhat larger meeting of senior officials convened by Robert Kennedy in the Situation

---

[35] Abel at 94–6. Sorensen's account of the same meeting is generally similar, although he does not mention Stevenson by name. Sorensen at 695–6. He says 'There was not a hint of "appeasing the aggressor" in these plans as some would charge, only an effort to propose a negotiating position perferable to war and acceptable to the world.' See also Kennedy at 49–50.

Room at the White House on Sunday night.[36] If the missiles were to be given up anyway, it might make sense, from the viewpoint of U.N. planning, to offer that concession to gain a tactical advantage in the Security Council. The other suggestions seemed to present similar possibilities.

This, in any event, was the line of argument that underlay the proposals. They were rejected ultimately, I believe, not because they added up to a Munich, but because, despite their superficial attractiveness, it turned out after study that they had even graver tactical disadvantages. They suffered from the defects of all anticipatory defences: one could not be sure in advance they would really be responsive to the claims or demands that would be made. There was the difficulty of formulating the proposals in the specific text of a resolution. The more general ideas being considered, such as, for example, the nuclear-free zone, posed problems of draftsmanship that did not seem possible to resolve in the time available. All of the proposals would have required consultation with other affected parties. The United States could hardly propose limitations on nuclear arms in Latin America or drastic changes in the Turkish defence posture without talking to these allies first. Even if there had been time and personnel for this purpose, the requirements of secrecy precluded any such discussions. Finally, the more one considered the tactic of offering concessions the more it seemed, not reasonable and forthcoming, but rather weak and defensive. It was inconsistent with the sense of resolution and determination that was judged essential to the success of the quarantine.

After several attempts to develop this approach in detail, with repeated and not unfriendly review by Secretary Rusk, it was finally abandoned in the late afternoon of Sunday.[37] All concerned, including, I believe, Ambassador Stevenson, agreed that it did not meet the immediate tactical needs of the situation as whole. The ideas were not rejected in principle. Many of the people who were there thought that they would have to return to a consideration of these and similar ideas before the crisis was over.

The alternative to making some kind of affirmative proposals

[36] I was personally present at this meeting.

[37] My own recollection is corroborated by the account in Schlesinger, n. 9 *supra*, at 810–11, which makes it clear that the final decisions on the U.N. position were made on Sunday.

for settlement was to call upon the Security Council to judge and condemn the Soviet Union. A resolution of this tenor was drafted by the group and introduced on Tuesday.[38] It reasserted the United States demand 'for immediate dismantling and withdrawal from Cuba of all missiles and other offensive weapons' and the dispatch to Cuba of a 'United Nations observer corps to assure and report on compliance'. Only after the affirmative 'certification of compliance' would the quarantine be terminated. The call for withdrawal of the missiles was expressly said to be 'under Article 40', that is a 'decision' of the Council having binding force under Article 25. The resolution stood no chance of being adopted and was not introduced with an expectation that it would be. It was the basis for a United States holding action in the U.N.

The Soviet resolution[39] was a mirror image, and it too was not put forward as a practical basis for Council action. It condemned 'the actions of the Government of the United States of America' and called for immediate revocation of the 'decision to inspect ships of other States bound for the Republic of Cuba' and for an end to 'any kind of interference in the internal affairs of the Republic of Cuba'. The only area of overlap between the two draft resolutions was a call for bilateral negotiations between the United States and the Soviet Union to remove the threat to peace and security.

I thought at the time and still believe that the course pursued in the U.N. was more consistent, on the whole, with the over-all requirements of United States policy than the alternatives proposed by Stevenson. But as might have been expected, our U.N. tactics failed to prevent a standstill proposal. As the crisis unrolled, with both Security Council and Assembly immobilized, U Thant exercised his initiative as Acting Secretary-General. In a letter to Kennedy and Khrushchev, he called for the 'voluntary suspension of all arms shipments to Cuba and also the voluntary suspension of the quarantine . . . for a period of two or three weeks . . .'.[40] What is more, the United States was not able to reject this appeal completely! On Friday 26 October, just after

---

[38] 17 U.N. SCOR, 1022d Meeting 16, U.N. Doc. S/5182 (1962).

[39] Id. at 36. U.N. Doc. S/5187.

[40] Letter of Acting Secretary-General U Thant to President Kennedy and Premier Khrushchev, dated 24 Oct. 1962, 17 U.N. SCOR, 1024th Meeting 21 (1962), also printed in Kennedy at 181.

the first and only interception of a Cuba-bound freighter by the United States navy, President Kennedy replied:

If the Soviet Government accepts and abides by your request that 'Soviet ships already on their way to Cuba . . . stay away from the interception area' for the limited time required for preliminary discussion you may be assured that this government will accept and abide by your request that our vessels in the Caribbean 'do everything possible to avoid direct confrontation with Soviet ships in the next few days in order to minimize the risk of any incident'.[41]

This undertaking was given before there was any agreement about withdrawing the missiles and while construction was still proceeding at the missile sites. True, it came after 'the other fellow blinked',[42] in Secretary Rusk's phrase. Many of the Soviet vessels thought to be carrying missiles had stopped or changed course, although some, as the President reminded the Secretary-General, were 'still proceeding toward Cuba and the interception area'.[43] No one can say, moreover, what would have happened to the President's undertaking if the settlement had not materialized on Sunday. It was limited in terms to 'the next few days' and to 'our vessels in the Caribbean'. Nevertheless, it represented an acceptance by the United States of something not unlike the asymmetrical standstill that the United States planners had feared and that had stimulated the proposal for a forthcoming U.N. strategy.

There was another aspect to the role of the U.N. in the crisis, neither neutral nor adverse to the United States objectives. The U.N., by its existence as an entity, provided a unique forum for crystallizing and mobilizing the views of governments and the public about the events. The antagonists faced each other in a glare of world publicity. The capacity of the U.N. to consume T.V. time during a crisis seems almost unlimited. For many states, the primary source of information was the reporting of their representatives in New York.

The debate on the Cuban missiles provided a striking demonstration of the significance of such a forum—and one of the most

[41] Letter from President Kennedy to Acting Secretary-General U Thant, dated 26 Oct. 1962, II Pan American Union, Inter-American Treaty of Reciprocal Assistance Applications 124–5 (1964), also printed in Kennedy at 189 (where it is misdated 25 Oct. 1962).

[42] Abel at 153; Hilsman at 215–6.

[43] Letter from President Kennedy to Acting Secretary-General U Thant, dated 26 Oct. 1962, n. 41 *supra*.

dramatic moments of the crisis as well—in the confrontation between Stevenson and Zorin on the floor of the Council[44] Zorin's ambiguous denial that missiles had been emplaced in Cuba, Stevenson's fury as he demanded a yes or no answer, the display of the enlarged U-2 photographs in the well of the Council, and Zorin's incredibly lame reply—all these together had a visible impact on the delegates, the governments they represented, and the publics that stood behind those governments. The episode was as effective in generating support for and neutralizing opposition to the United States as any other action in the week of the crisis.[45]

iv

In addition to the practical and operational consequences just described, the organizational setting provided the doctrinal basis of the legal analysis put forward by the United States. For scholars of international law, that may be as important an impact as any other.

The legal approach of the United States did not, on the whole, seek to identify rules or norms of conduct and to analyse these by the familiar techniques of legal reasoning to show that they were or were not applicable to the situation. The central concepts in the debate—'armed attack' in Article 51, 'threat to the peace, breach of the peace or act of aggression' in Article 39, 'fact or situation that might endanger the peace of America' in Article 6 of the Rio Treaty—all these are treated by the United States analysis as essentially political categories. They provide broad, general guides to political decision, but they are not susceptible to much elaboration or refinement by legal techniques.

The basic legal problem presented by the crisis, in this view, was not the development of authoritative and generally applicable definitions of these terms. The legal problem was to determine which of the actors and entities on the international scene was empowered to make the political decisions that these phrases proffered, given the structure and interrelationships of the organizations involved. On what questions and in what circumstances was decision in the first instance allotted to the individual state acting unilaterally? As to which issues is competence vested in the

---

[44] 17 U.N. SCOR, 1025th Meeting, 2–17 (1962).
[45] See, e.g., Schlesinger, n. 9 *supra*, at 824; Kennedy at 75–6.

regional organization and as to which is it in the U.N.? In each case, by what organs and procedures is the authority to be exercised? What are the relations between the actions of a state and those of the international organization? When and how does one pre-empt, displace, or supersede another?

Critics of the United States position have often failed to recognize this shift from the traditional focus. For example, one of them argues:

> ... if the Rio Treaty was valid and if the peace and security of the Continent were endangered, then the quarantine was legal. However, those are rather large 'ifs', and the reasoning was not accepted by all and perhaps not even most of those persons around the world with any reasonable claim to be called international lawyers.[46]

But the two 'ifs' raise very different kinds of questions. Whether the Rio Treaty was 'valid', in the sense of authorizing the kinds of decisions taken by the O.A.S., is a central structural question, and the United States Memorandum tries to deal with it. Whether a situation 'might endanger the peace of America' is a political question, on which the judgment of international lawyers is not entitled to any particular weight. The Rio Treaty did not set up a *standard* permitting an objective conclusion on that issue by the method of reason. It established a process for deciding the question by the method of politics.

I have emphasized elsewhere that the salient characteristic of international law is that it deals with governmental behaviour.[47] It is, in my view, a naïve oversimplification to suppose that public law can establish codes of 'conduct' for governmental entities in anything approaching the way private law does so for individuals. In the United States we have some experience, still not too extensive and not all happy, with the application of normative rules to government by the method of law. Elsewhere there is almost none. Government action is held within bounds, if at all, by other agencies than law.

But we are very familiar with law that deals with sovereign power in a different way, by establishing jurisdictions and al-

---

[46] Gerberding, 'International Law and the Cuban Missile Crisis', in Scheinman and Wilkinson (eds.), *International Law and Political Crisis* 175, 183 (1969).

[47] Chayes, 'A Common Lawyer Looks at International Law', 79 Harv. L. Rev. 1396 (1965).

locating decision-making powers. This branch of constitutional law carries with it a special professional tradition and method. In the main, its object has not been to secure 'right' answers to substantive questions. It has been to ensure that the decision of a class of great public questions is remitted to the institution whose competence, procedures, and structure give assurance that it will make wise decision on those questions.

That it was correct to pose the legal issues in the Cuban missile crisis in those terms, I have little doubt. If international law is to deal, as it must, with 'power that comes close to the sources of sovereignty' it must do so not in the form of rules of conduct but by means of constitutional architecture.

VI

FINAL CLAUSES

i

IT is widely maintained that the United States would have attacked Cuba on Monday, or Tuesday at the latest, if the U.S.S.R. had not accepted the terms offered it. Many believe that this is why the Soviets capitulated.[1] Allison summarizes as follows the conclusion of what he calls 'perhaps the most careful sustained strategic analysis of the crisis':[2]

Khrushchev withdrew the Soviet missiles not because of the blockade, not because of the implicit threat of 'further action', but because of an *explicit* threat of air strike or invasion on Tuesday—unless he served immediate notice that the missiles would be withdrawn.[3]

What relevance has all of this to an assessment of the role of law in the crisis?

Technically, the same argument that was used in the first week to support the quarantine would have been available in the second week to defend an air strike or invasion. The O.A.S. resolution authorized member-states to take

... all measures, individually and collectively, which they may deem necessary to ensure that the Government of Cuba cannot continue to receive from the Sino-Soviet powers military material and related supplies which may threaten the peace and security of the Continent and to prevent the missiles in Cuba from ever becoming an active threat to the peace and security of the Continent.[4]

This language is not limited to naval action to prevent missiles from arriving in Cuba; it covers as well air strike and invasion against missiles already there. It was deliberately drafted that way. And there can be little doubt that the O.A.S., or at least the representatives in the Organ of Consultation, so understood it. The point was made explicitly in debate, and, as we have

---

[1] See Allison at 62–6.
[2] Id., at 63.   [3] Id., at 65.
[4] OEA/Ser. C/II/C-a-463 (1962), 47 Dep't of State Bull. 723 (1962).

seen, was the ground upon which some countries abstained in the clause-by-clause vote that preceded the final unanimous adoption of the resolution as a whole.[5]

Nevertheless, Professor Henkin, a moderate and perceptive commentator, suggests that bombing or invasion of Cuba at that stage would have amounted to 'serious violations of law . . .'.[6] If so, this willingness of the United States 'to court the cost and consequence'[7] would reflect back on the claims of law with respect to the entire decision-process.

There is no doubt that the qualities of restraint and proportion, which lent substance and credibility to the United States legal case, would have been seriously compromised by a full-scale appeal to force. McDougal, who was prepared to rely on Article 51 in support of the blockade, nevertheless insisted that any legal rationale must recognize 'the basic constitutional policies of necessity and proportionality'.[8] We have already suggested that some such limitation was implicit in Meeker's exposition before the Executive Committee, which he confined to the case for a 'defensive quarantine'.[9]

In the circumstances, it may seem that the issue of whether there would have been an attack on Cuba is best relegated to the realm of 'iffy' questions. But though that may be the better part of valour, it does not leave our analysis in very satisfactory shape. Some further speculation seems warranted.

Speculation must begin with the admission that major escalation in the second week was a substantial possibility. The forces had been in place for a week: 200,000 assault troops in Florida and squadrons of tactical aircraft at bases in south-eastern states within effective range of Cuba. On Saturday, 24 troop-carrier squadrons of the Air Force Reserve were called to active duty.[10]

Pressures within the government for an attack were formidable. Allison says:

By Thursday evening, most members of the ExCom saw the blockade was not working: while it prevented Soviet missile shipments to Cuba,

---

[5] See p. 74 *supra*.
[6] Henkin, *How Nations Behave* 227, n. † (1968).
[7] Ibid.
[8] McDougal, 'The Soviet–Cuban Quarantine and Self-Defense', 57 Am. J. Int'l L. 597, 603 n. 14 (1963).
[9] See p. 146 *supra*, and n. 34, p. 15.
[10] See Allison at 64.

construction of missiles already on the island rushed toward operational readiness. Thus they faced the issue of the next step.[11]

Advocates of harsher action, particularly the military, renewed their attack. According to Robert Kennedy, the Joint Chiefs recommended

. . . an air strike on Monday, followed shortly afterward by an invasion. They pointed out to the President that they had always felt the blockade to be far too weak a course and that military steps were the only ones the Soviet Union would understand. They were not at all surprised that nothing had been achieved by limited force, for this is exactly what they had predicted.[12]

The force with which these views were pressed can be seen in General LeMay's suggestion, after the settlement, that the United States should attack on Monday in any case.[13] Robert Kennedy says

. . . the feeling grew that this cup was not going to pass and that a direct military confrontation between the two great nuclear powers was inevitable. . . . If the Russians continued to be adamant and continued to build up their missile strength, military force would be the only alternative.[14]

Elaborate preparations for invasion were ordered: printing of Spanish-language-leaflets, planning for civil government, preparation of a roster of Cuban doctors in Miami.[15]

The threat was conveyed explicitly to the Soviets. On Saturday evening, Robert Kennedy saw Ambassador Dobrynin to deliver the President's crucial letter to Khrushchev. In this, the most direct and secure channel of communication between the two

[11] Id., at 219.

[12] Kennedy at 96–7; see also Abel at 192–3.

[13] Allison at 206. The same attitude is suggested in the story recounted by Abel of General Taylor's reaction to Robert Kennedy's moral reservations about a surprise attack: 'Maxwell Taylor, seemingly impressed by the speech of Robert Kennedy, agreed that a surprise attack was out of the question. "Max is a moral man", one participant recalls. "He showed what a moral man he is by recommending that we give the Cubans twenty-four hours advance notice—and then strike the missile bases." ' Abel at 88. Allison argues that from the standpoint of the military services, the whole crisis was seen as an occasion for the 'elimination of the Communist Cuban thorn'. Allison at 124–5.

[14] Kennedy at 83.

[15] Id. at 85; Allison at 219.

heads of government in the crisis, the Attorney General told the Ambassador:

> We had to have a commitment by tomorrow that those bases would be removed. I was not giving them an ultimatum but a statement of fact. He should understand that if they did not remove those bases, we would remove them. . . .
>
> Time was running out. We had only a few more hours—we needed an answer immediately from the Soviet Union. I said we must have it the next day.[16]

There is no reason to suppose that the Soviets ignored these warnings. Krushchev reported to the Supreme Soviet:

> We received information from Cuban comrades and from other sources on the morning of [Saturday] October 27 directly stating that this attack would be carried out in the next two or three days. We interpreted these cables as an extremely alarming warning signal.[17]

Certainly the Kremlin would have been imprudent to say the least, to have concluded that all these preparations and warnings were bluff.

Even one who believes, as I do, that the President would not have countenanced further armed action as a matter of deliberate decision, must concede the considerable possibility of escalation by accident—of things getting out of hand. Thomas Schelling has drawn attention to 'The Threat that Leaves Something to Chance'.[18]

> The key to these threats is that, though one may or may not carry them out if the threatened party fails to comply, *the final decision is not altogether under the threatener's control.* . . .
>
> Where does the uncertain element in the decision come from? It must come from somewhere outside of the threatener's control. Whether we call it 'chance', accident, third-party influence, imperfection in the machinery of decision, or just processes that we do not entirely understand, it is an ingredient in the situation that neither we nor the party we threaten can entirely control. An example is the threat of inadvertent war.[19]

[16] Kennedy at 108–9.

[17] Allison at 64–5, quoting the *N.Y. Times*, 14 Dec. 1962. Robert Kennedy's visit to Dobrynin was on the night of the 27th, so that Khrushchev's reference cannot be to this encounter. Perhaps the 'other sources' included John Scali who was approached by the Soviet Embassy in Washington and delivered a tough message to his contact on Friday night, 26 Oct. See Hilsman at 217–18.

[18] Schelling, *The Strategy of Conflict*, chap. 8 (1963).

[19] Id. at 188.

This description seems to fit perfectly the threat implicit in the situation as the week ground on. Certainly this sense of constant pressure against the limits of control dominated the minds of the principals, Kennedy and Khrushchev, and each tried to emphasize this aspect for the other.

. . . As Soviet ships approached the quarantine line, the American leaders sent a letter to the Soviets expressing concern 'that we both show prudence and do nothing to allow events to *make the situation more difficult to control than it is*'. Later a Soviet reply emphasized the danger, 'Contact of our ships . . . can spark off the fire of military conflict after which any talks would be superfluous because other forces and other laws would begin to operate—the *laws of war.*' As the climax of the crisis drew near, developments were, in the American phrase 'approaching a point where *events could have become unmanageable*'. The Russians chose another metaphor: the logic of war. 'If indeed war should break out, then it would not be in our power to stop it, for such is the logic of war.'[20]

Allison concludes, in fact, that in some respects the main contest of the crisis was not external—government against government—but internal—'government leaders against organizations whose outputs they sought to control'.[21]

Evidence that something—and perhaps a good bit more—was left to chance abounds in the events of the first week. A U-2, for example, wandered off course and into Soviet air space. Russian fighters had taken off before the pilot got back on course. The incident produced one of the most memorable JFK quotes of the crisis: 'There is always some son-of-a-bitch who doesn't get the word.' But, as the President knew, the possible consequences of such a mistake were catastrophic.[22] Or, as another example, on Tuesday 23 October, the Executive Committee had decided that in the event of a U-2 being shot down over Cuba, the United States would retaliate by bombing a SAM battery. On Saturday, the SAMs became operational and did in fact bring down a U-2. The President, however, decided to defer the retaliatory attack.

A . . . member of the ExCom recalled that the Air Force might have taken the Tuesday decision as authorization to proceed with the retaliation. A series of rapid calls just managed to intercept Air Force implementation of what it had taken to be 'orders' . . .[23]

[20] Allison at 132; see also id. at 212.
[21] Id. at 132.   [22] Id. at 141.   [23] Id. at 140.

These examples could be multiplied. Any one of them—or a thousand others—might have sparked military action.

Against this formidable array of evidence, what case can be made that the President and his closest advisers would have resisted the pressures, and barring accident, would have found a way to resolve the crisis short of war.

First, all the accounts emphasize the President's deep and passionate appreciation of the full consequences and horrors of nuclear war. The President's brother gives a particularly moving and convincing portrayal of the President's state of mind in the final desperate hours:

... It was not only for Americans that he was concerned or primarily for the older generation of any land. The thought that disturbed him most, and that made the prospect of war much more fearful than it could otherwise have been, was the specter of the death of the children of this country and all the world—the young people who had no role, who had no say, who knew nothing even of the confrontation, but whose lives would be snuffed out like everyone else's . . .[24]

Allison concludes:

The burden of responsibility for actually *making* judgments that might cause the quick death of millions of human beings and the destruction of entire societies must have been overwhelming. While he could involve others in the choice, his was the responsibility for the outcome. This qualitative difference in responsibility must have exaggerated the differences between his perspective and that of the men around him.[25]

In fact, Allison says, Kennedy shared this unique perspective with only one other man: Khrushchev. And this led him 'to become the guardian within his own government, of his "partner's perspective and problem" '.[26]

Second, the President's initial reaction when he heard about the missiles was that an invasion or strike of some sort was required.[27] Every move he made thereafter, however, was in the direction of further restraint and deferral of violence. He shifted from strike to quarantine.[28] He put off the effective date of the

---

[24] Kennedy at 106.
[25] Allison at 211.
[26] Id. at 213.
[27] See Abel at 49; Allison at 202.
[28] Sorensen at 691; Allison at 205.

quarantine to Wednesday.[29] He let two ships through the line without challenge and carefully selected the vessel that was to be stopped, with a view to its acquiescing.[30] When the SAMs shot down the U-2 he deferred the retaliatory strike already decided upon.[31] He cancelled low-level reconnaissance flights, for fear they could draw fire, although these had been initiated as a device to intensify pressure on the antagonists.[32] This is not the picture of a man engaged in a test of wills to be pursued to the end, but of one anxious to avoid an armed engagement at any acceptable cost. Indeed there were many in the government who, upon hearing of these decisions, believed the President had caved in.[33]

Third, on Saturday and Sunday morning, heated debate continued among senior officials, including members of the Executive Committee, about whether to add POL (petroleum, oil, and lubricants) to the list of quarantined items. No decision had been reached when the news of the settlement arrived.[34] This was the only item whose interdiction might ultimately have had a severe impact within Cuba. It hardly seems possible that it would have been easier to authorize an attack than intensification of the blockade.

Finally, there is the question of the Turkish missiles. Here from the very beginning was a key to a settlement. Thomas Schelling's discussion of bargaining between parties with both common and conflicting interests stresses the significance of 'clues or co-ordinators or focal points'.[35]

If we then ask what it is that can . . . bring the negotiation to a close, we might propose that it is the intrinsic magnetism of particular outcomes, especially those that enjoy prominence, uniqueness, simplicity, precedent, or some rationale that makes them qualitatively differentiable from the continum of possible alternatives.[36]

The Cuba–Turkey exchange had all the characteristics of such a focal point.

---

[29] Interdiction of the Delivery of Offensive Weapons to Cuba, Proclamation No. 3504, 23 Oct. 1962, 27 Fed. Reg. 10401 (1962).
[30] See Allison at 128–30.
[31] Id. at 140.
[32] Ibid.   [33] Ibid.
[34] Abel at 199; I was a participant in these discussions.
[35] Schelling. n. 18 *supra*, at 57.
[36] Id. at 70.

It was first proposed by Stevenson on Saturday 20 October, and rejected, at least for openers.[37] But at a meeting of senior officials, including a number of members of the Executive Committee, the night before the President's speech, Robert McNamara had said we would be lucky to get out of the crisis with only a trade of the Turkish missiles. In response to Robert Kennedy's direct question to every person at the table, there was no disagreement with McNamara's evaluation.[38]

In the United States, the first significant public linkage of Cuban with Turkish missiles was in Walter Lippmann's column on Thursday morning, three days after the President's speech. But the suggestion that the parallel between the two forward deployments might provide the basis of a bargain had been in the London papers from Tuesday on,[39] and prominent in U.N. corridor talk from the beginning. Lippmann's column outlined the rationale for such an exchange in some detail. He urged an effort

... to negotiate a face-saving agreement.

I hasten to say at once that I am not talking about, and do not believe in, a 'Cuba–Berlin' horse trade. Cuba and Berlin are wholly different cases. Berlin is not an American missile base. It is not a base for any kind of offensive, as Cuba is by way of becoming.

The only place that is truly comparable with Cuba is Turkey. This is the only place where there are strategic missiles right on the frontier of the Soviet Union . . .

There is another important similarity between Cuba and Turkey. The Soviet missile base in Cuba, like the US–NATO base in Turkey, is of little military value. The Soviet military base in Cuba is defenseless and the base in Turkey is all but obsolete. The two bases could be dismantled without altering the world balance of power.[40]

Whether or not the Russians viewed it as a trial balloon from the White House, Lippmann's proposal, reinforced as it was by discussion in many other quarters, had 'prominence' and 'conspicuousness'. He was in the position of one of Schelling's mediators, who

---

[37] See pp. 80–1 *supra*.

[38] See pp. 81–2 *supra*.

[39] See *The Times*, 24 Oct. 1962 (editorial); cf. the *Guardian*, 23 Oct. 1962 (editorial).

[40] *Washington Post*, 25 Oct. 1962 p. A-25, col. 1.

... often display a power to precipitate agreement and a power to determine the terms of agreement; their proposals often seem to be accepted less by reason of their inherent fairness or reasonableness, than by a kind of resignation of both participants ... it is not the facts themselves but the creation of a specific suggestion, that seems to exercise the influence.[41]

Moreover, in this case, as Robert Kennedy was to acknowledge in retrospect, the Cuba–Turkey exchange 'was not unreasonable and did not amount to a loss to the US or to our NATO allies'.[42] And to cap it all, as Lippmann said, the Turkish missiles were obsolete. The President had been trying to get rid of them almost from the day he took office.[43]

In these circumstances, is it conceivable that John F. Kennedy would have permitted these few obsolete weapons to stand in the way of a peaceful settlement? What was the argument against the trade? In rejecting Stevenson's proposals a week earlier, the President had said that

... this was not the time for concessions that could wreck Western alliance, seeming to confirm the suspicion that Charles de Gaulle had planted that the United States would sacrifice the interests of its allies to protect its own security.[44]

Macmillan gives Kennedy high marks for refusing 'against the advice of weaker brethren in America and elsewhere, to bargain the security of the western world by yielding to the specious Russian offers of a face-saving accommodation at the expense of America's allies'.[45]

No doubt these considerations were significant in moulding the

[41] Schelling, n. 18 *supra*, at 68.
[42] Kennedy at 94.
[43] See, e.g., Allison at 141–3; Kennedy at 94–5. Allison's account as well as others leave the impression that the President was unaware that his earlier orders had not been carried out and was angered to discover that the missiles were still in Turkey. It may well be that he was angry. But as one who had some part in the efforts to carry out those earlier orders, I cannot believe he was surprised. The delays and obstacles in withdrawing the Turkish and Italian missiles had been fully and currently reported to him. When the Cuban crisis began, he and other members of the Executive Committee were aware of the status of these weapons. Retaliation against Turkey because of the missiles there was considered a possible Soviet response to any United States action from the outset. See Sorensen at 680.
[44] Abel at 95; see p. 80 *supra*, Sorensen at 696.
[45] Kennedy at 19 (Introduction by Harold Macmillan).

United States opening position. As we saw earlier, it would have been anomalous to offer concessions at the very beginning without having any chance to see what the reactions of the Soviets or anyone else would be. Moreover, in the beginning an offer to exchange the Turkish missiles would necessarily have been unilateral, without consultation with the Turks or other NATO allies. Even if we assume that the countries concerned might have been delighted to be rid of the affair on these terms, it is equally true that unilateral action by the United States would have rankled long after the crisis had faded.

As the week wore on, however, and especially on Saturday after the Soviets formally offered a Cuba–Turkey settlement, the picture changed. Consultation with the Turks was now possible so that now to reject the Soviet offer would carry a taint of unilateralism. The President himself raised the issue:

... What role should Turkey and the rest of NATO have in determining our responses. Within a very short time, they might be faced with decisions of life and death. Before that happened should they not have a right to learn, if not pass on, what we were deciding to do, particularly if that was likely to affect them in such a rapid and possibly devastating way.

... NATO was supporting the United States, but were these countries truly and completely aware of the dangers for them.[46]

Official support in the alliance seemed to be holding firm. But among ordinary citizens there were surely doubts. British newspapers of all political shades had been urging the dismantling of the Turkish missiles as a basis for settlement from the first announcement of the crisis.[47] The Labour Party issued a statement critical of the United States action and barely held silent in the Parliamentary debates on the issue.[48] On Sunday 28 October, the day the settlement was concluded, The Times of London urged editorially that the Soviet offer to trade Cuban for Turkish missiles should be accepted.[49]

As for Turkey, the special status that the presence of Jupiters carried with it may have led it to resist their removal when there was no serious danger. It is quite another thing to suppose that

[46] Kennedy at 98–9.
[47] The Times, 24 Oct. 1962 (editorial), 26 Oct. 1962 (editorial); Guardian, 23 Oct. 1962 (editorial), 24 Oct. 1962 (editorial), 25 Oct. 1962 (editorial).
[48] See The Times, 25 Oct. 1962, p. 10, col. 4; 26 Oct. 1962, p. 6, col. 6.
[49] Id., 28 Oct. 1962 (editorial).

Ankara would have demurred if it had been consulted at the height of the crisis. It is hard to believe that the Turks were very anxious for the honour of being the first nuclear target since the Second World War.

How is this conflict of evidence and supposition to be resolved? Allison argues that *the President actually did accept the Soviet offer*. In his view, Khrushchev's agreement to withdraw the missiles was not simply a capitulation to superior American force. He interprets the conversation between Robert Kennedy and Soviet Ambassador Dobrynin on Saturday night as evidence of a 'deal', a tacit assurance that the Turkish missiles would be withdrawn.[50] Kennedy records the conversation as follows:

He [Dobrynin] raised the question of our removing the missiles from Turkey. I said that there could be no quid pro quo or any arrangement made under this kind of threat or pressure, and that in the last analysis this was a decision that would have to be made by NATO. However, I said, President Kennedy had been anxious to remove those missiles from Turkey and Italy for a long period of time. He had ordered their removal some time ago, and it was our judgment that, within a short time after the crisis was over, those missiles would be gone.[51]

In point of fact, they were removed within six months.[52]

Allison's interpretation strikes me as wholly reasonable. But even if it is wrong, or if the Soviets had insisted on a more public assurance, there is a ground for supposing that a way would have been found to meet the requirement if it had been necessary to avoid further armed action. Abel describes the Executive Committee meeting on Saturday morning, after the Soviet offer arrived:

... The free-wheeling discussion that Saturday canvassed every possible approach short of submitting to Khrushchev's demand. Although Stevenson has since been identified as the chief advocate, men with

---

[50] Allison at 218, 228–30; see id. at 226, however, for a review of all the statements that any such 'deal' was unacceptable.

[51] Kennedy at 108–9.

[52] An interdepartmental task force on removal of these missiles was convened on Monday morning, 29 Oct., the day after the settlement, under the chairmanship of John McNaughton, General Counsel of the Department of Defense. He opened the meeting with the statement, 'Those missiles are going to be out of there by April 1 if we have to shoot them out.' The actual date of removal was 15 April. The same fire-power was maintained, however, by stationing additional Polaris submarines in the Mediterranean.

established reputations for cold-war toughness turned their minds that afternoon to ingenious devices for removing the Turkish missiles from the equation without seeming to accept Khrushchev's terms. There was talk round the table of a maneuver by which the Turkish Government would somehow be persuaded to petition the United States for their removal. Finally, the discussion settled on a new concept. The Executive Committee agreed that the United States could afford to pay a considerable price in subsequent negotiations if the Russians would stop their Cuba missile build-up at once, before the IRBM's became operational. The concession was to be disguised as part of a broader negotiation with the Russians concerning relaxation of tensions between NATO and the Warsaw Pact. Accordingly, the President talked privately with Rusk and McNamara at the close of the morning session and then assigned Gilpatric to spend the afternoon in Bundy's basement office at the White House, with representatives of the State Department and the Joint Chiefs of Staff, writing a 'scenario' for the early removal of all Jupiter missiles from Turkey and Italy. There were to be two separate plans in view of the differing national circumstances as between Turks and Italians. Gilpatric's scenario was to be ready for the Executive Committee's third meeting of the day at 9 P.M.[53]

Abel links 'this unreported decision accepting the removal of the Jupiter bases as a legitimate goal of subsequent negotiations' with a public statement issued that afternoon stressing the possibility of wider negotiations once the Cuban missiles had been removed.[54] Decisions about the Turkish missiles went beyond the stage of writing scenarios. The President ordered that the atomic warheads should be defused. Robert Kennedy says this was to ensure that the President 'personally would have to give permission before they were used'.[55] Allison, basing his account on personal interviews with participants, goes further and suggests that the President 'decided to withdraw American missiles from Turkey in order to remove the target that the Soviet Union could legitimately strike when the United States performed the hard actions that would have to be chosen on Sunday'.[56]

Both explanations have their difficulties. The Jupiters were soft, exposed weapons. Their only use was in a first strike. To defuse them was to give the President assurance that they would not be fired, but not much possibility for using them, if it came to that. It was tantamount to taking them 'off the board', as the President is said to have ordered in anger that Saturday after-

---

[53] Abel at 194–5.   [54] Id. at 195.
[55] Kennedy at 98.   [56] Allison at 142.

noon.[57] As for Allison's explanation, if the President was ready to withdraw the missiles to eliminate a target, why not to make a deal?

One group in the government had no difficulty interpreting the President's actions:

To a number of others, particularly the military who were present or who learned of the decision [to defuse the missiles] as the meeting was debriefed by staffs in the Pentagon and elsewhere, the point was clear: the President had cracked and folded.[58]

That is, he was prepared to settle.

Whether, if agreement had not been reached on Sunday, the President would have ordered an attack on Monday or Tuesday remains unknowable, like so much else that might clarify the enigma of John F. Kennedy. There is no doubt that this impression was forcefully conveyed to the Soviets. There is little doubt that in so doing significant risks of inadvertent war were deliberately created. I do not think it can be convincingly demonstrated, however, that the President and his closest advisers were prepared to abandon abruptly 'the basic constitutional policies of necessity and proportion' they had so sedulously maintained to that point in the crisis.[59]

ii

A study of the role of law in the Cuban missile crisis inevitably seems to exaggerate that role. The meetings of the Executive Committee were not dominated by debates on fine points of law. Nor would one have wished that they should be.

The factual record is irrefutable, however, that the men responsible for decision did not ignore legal considerations. On the contrary, they made a considerable effort to integrate legal factors into their deliberations. The President and his advisers were properly concerned with the possibilities—for good or ill— in the situation they faced and in the courses open to them. Law

[57] Ibid.; see also id. at 227.

[58] Id. at 142.

[59] Sorensen says, also, that 'The President would not, in my judgment, have moved immediately to either an air strike or an invasion; . . .' But he adds that pressures in that direction were growing 'rapidly and irresistibly'. Sorensen at 715–16.

and legal institutions played a part in defining and shaping those possibilities.

This much can be said with some confidence about the role of law in the Cuban missile crisis. It remains to restate, though in necessarily tentative form, some more general conclusions that have emerged about the operation of law in crisis decision-making.

Understanding is obscured by two transparent but pervasive misconceptions—one about the nature of law and one about the character of the decision-process. Both are expressions of what I have called the anthropomorphic fallacy. In both law is cast as the superego setting outer limits to permissible action.

But decision-making is *not* a wholly integrated and rational activity. It embodies large elements of misperception, faulty evaluation, miscalculation, failure of communication. These are not occasional or sporadic lapses in an essentially rational exercise. They are massive and they are endemic. Most important, decision-making is a *corporate* process in which individual participants react to different constellations of personal, bureaucratic, and political motives and constraints. All this must be taken into account in any serious effort to understand or explain how the process works.

And law is *not* a set of fixed, self-defining categories of permissible and prohibited conduct. This conception is invalid even as to domestic law, but it is especially so as to international law because of the diffuse modes of establishing and clarifying rules. Its assumptions about the relation of law to decision are reminiscent of Justice Robert's idea of constitutional adjudication. 'The Court', he said, 'has only one duty—to lay the article of the Constitution which is invoked beside the statute which is challenged and to see whether the latter squares with the former.' [60] Supreme Court Justices and their critics have long since abandoned this mechanistic approach. But there are many who still consider that legal advice or criticism in the international field consists in laying the norm invoked beside the challenged decision and seeing whether the latter squares with the former.

International law, in its normative sense, must be seen as indeterminate with respect to much of the array of concrete choices open in a particular situation. Often the rules have no authoritative formulation in words. Even when they do, the

[60] *United States* v. *Butler*, 297 U.S. 1, 62 (1936).

terms are open to a broad range of interpretation and emphasis. They do not dictate conduct so much as orient deliberation, order priorities, guide within broad limits. Moreover, institutional structures that are the product of law can be as important as rules, and more so in organizing and channelling decision.

These more complex concepts of law and decision-making can lead to a richer appreciation of the complicated interplay between the two. Four salient points emerge from this study:

First, law is not self-activating. On the whole, it does not project itself into the deliberations on its own motion. Someone must call the lawyers in. The Cuban missile crisis seems to authenticate a traditional stereotype: in the course of an orderly canvass of considerations relevant to decision, and after the major alternatives had been clarified, government lawyers were asked to present, to the inner circle of decision-makers, a formal exposition of the legal situation and the legal constraints. But our study suggests that this is not the whole story. The impact of the legal presentation will depend on how much time is available for careful and considered development and how early and how insistently it is put before the responsible operating officers. This in turn depends on factors that condition *all* lawyer–client relations, public and private. How do the legal offices fit into the particular bureaucratic structures involved? What are the personal relations between the lawyer and his immediate client? We saw that there were differences in both dimensions as between Defense and State. How does the legal officer view his role? Like the Attorney General, as an active participant in the policy-making process? Or does he wait for questions to be put to him, and then answer only what he is asked? What is his skill in using his professional leverage?

Second, if legal precepts are not exogenous data, dividing the universe of choices into the permissible and impermissible, if legal analysis is always indeterminate, then at best legal reasoning and analysis will impact on alternatives in terms of more or less, not yes or no. Law cannot determine decision, and it is an essential point of this study that we should not expect it to. It takes its place as one of a complex of factors for sorting out available choices.

In return for shedding its oracular pretensions, legal analysis gains a continuous relevance at every point along the spectrum of potential decision. If it cannot divide the universe into mutually

exclusive blacks and whites, it can help in differentiating the
infinite shades of grey that are the grist of the decision-process.
The corporate character of decision-making ensures that these
differentiating considerations will be pressed home by the participants whose policy positions they favour. The persuasive force
of such arguments and their final influence will depend on infinitely complex moral, psychological, and interpersonal processes
of group decision-making. Quantification, as we have said, must
always elude us. But the position that the ultimate impact is
de minimis cannot be maintained.

  Third, the significance of legal justification for decision-making
is greater and more complex than is customarily supposed. Legal
justification is part of the over-all defence of a public decision. It
is easy to deprecate the significance of this process. Casual
observation is enough to show that public justification is not always
based on the 'real' reasons for decision, and may even falsify
them. But it is wrong to conclude on this basis that the decision
and its announced rationale are essentially independent and
self-contained phenomena.

  In fact, the requirement of justification suffuses the basic
process of choice. There is continuous feedback between the
knowledge that the government will be called upon to justify its
action and the kind of action that can be chosen. The linkage
tends to induce a tolerable congruence between the actual
corporate decision-process, with its interplay of personal, bureaucratic, and political factors, and the idealized picture of rational
choice on the basis of objectively coherent criteria. We may grant
a considerable latitude for evasion and manipulation. But to
ignore the requirement of justification too long or to violate its
canons too egregiously creates, in a democracy, what we have
come to call a 'credibility gap'. The ultimate consequence is to
erode the capacity of the government to govern.

  Some of the characteristics of law give it special importance for
public justification. Because of the scope and variety of the
audiences addressed, that process must proceed in terms of more
or less universal and generalized criteria. It cannot rely heavily
on the detailed factual knowledge, elaborate shared assumptions,
personal relations, professional expertise that may be persuasive
in internal bargaining over policy. For these reasons, ideological
elements, for example, tend to bulk large in public defence and
justification of policy. Legal principles also are regarded as quasi-

universal or at least generally accepted. They are thus well adapted to the needs of public justification. On the other hand, because of the very prominence of legal standards as criteria for public accounting, failure to justify on these grounds or an inadequate legal defence may compromise the justification exercise over-all. Law thus becomes a prominent element in the justification process.

Comparative justifiability—which is another way of saying the comparative ease of generating political support or acquiescence —is necessarily an important factor differentiating among available alternatives in the intra-governmental process of choice. The perhaps disproportionate significance of law for public justification feeds back on this internal process to enhance the weight of legal considerations there.

Fourth, decision must take account of the international organizational setting against which action is projected. Since the organizational setting is in the strict sense a product of international law, this amounts to identifying a major and continuing legal influence on decision. International institutions, moreover, are a focused and intensified arena of public justification. They are peculiarly sensitive to the legal elements of the position, because the organizations themselves are dominated by legalistic modes of procedure. Most important of all, the international organizations are themselves actors, with some power to create legal relations and alter the legal setting. From a narrowly national point of view, this means that action must be planned with an eye to controlling or neutralizing these actors. From the broader perspective of international law, these not wholly controllable international actors, responsive to legal argumentation and acting by law-created processes, are of increasing importance in the effort to channel national action.

In my view, these four factors are inherent in the structure of United States decision-making, certainly in the 1960s and probably since the Second World War, that is, ever since United States foreign-policy decisions have been consequential:

—lawyers, operating in a professional role, are found in all agencies of the national security bureaucracy;
—policy decision is significantly a bargaining process in which legal arguments, like all other available arguments, are used for what they are worth;

—the government acknowledges some duty of public justification of action;
—international organizations are a recognized feature of the setting of decision.

In combination, these factors work to enhance the role of law, and to ensure that legal considerations are present, to a degree, in any concrete instance of decision-making that occurs within the structure. To what degree is a matter of time, occasion, and persons. But I believe it is characteristically greater than is allowed for by most current theories of international relations.

It does not necessarily follow that the structural features referred to ensure that 'adequate' weight is given to legal considerations in United States decision-making past or present; still less that results are always to be approved from the standpoint of international law. These are questions if not of taste then at least on which informed judgments may differ.

iii

If our analysis produces little by way of quantitative or normative comfort, it at least generates some prescriptive propositions in which we can have considerable confidence. It is not hard to produce a practical programme of action for one seeking to increase the role of law in decisions on international questions (or to limit it).

—It makes a difference whether there is systematic provision within the principal responsible departments for consultation of lawyers in advance of decision and how far in advance; whether such consultation is treated as a routine bureaucratic function or as an occasion for policy influence; whether the lawyers themselves, particularly the chief legal officers, conceive their role as including active participation in political decision. The Department of Justice, as the chief law office of the government, and the Attorney General, as the chief law officer, have, potentially, a key role that is often overlooked. Its importance depends in part on the personal relation between the President and the Attorney General; but the role of the Secretary of State also depends on his relationship with the President.

—It makes a difference what attitude and policy the government adopts towards international organizations as a matter of course in quieter times. A habit of reliance on an international institution to deal with large political questions, even if only in debate, will increase the pressure for recourse to that institution at the crisis point. A policy that enlists the approbation and support of an international institution over time will create increasingly insistent expectations of continuing resort to the institutional processes.

—Finally, it makes a difference how far a governmental duty of public justification is acknowledged and enforced. Secret decisions by military and diplomatic professionals, based on asserted superior knowledge and expertise, and packaged under the label 'the President knows best'—this is not a hospitable setting for the operation of legal considerations.

The willingness of government to accept the obligation of legal justification in any particular instance makes that obligation harder to avoid the next time round. But as is the case with other inconvenient burdens, it is not enough to rely on the goodwill of those who must bear them. Whoever would enhance the role of international law in decision-making must strive to keep the demand for justification active and urgent—in the Congress, in the press, and in the longer time-frame of scholarship.

The requirement of justification is another name for public accountability. Its importance should not come as a surprise to people who set store by democratic processes. It should not be a surprise either—in a country whose policy is rooted in Lockian assumptions and whose tradition of judicial review ultimately turns every political question into a legal question[61]—that justification, whatever else it may include, means accountability before the law.

[61] I de Tocqueville, *Democracy in America* 280 (ed. Bradley, 1945).

APPENDIX I

MEMORANDUM FOR THE ATTORNEY GENERAL
RE: LEGALITY UNDER INTERNATIONAL LAW
OF REMEDIAL ACTION AGAINST USE OF
CUBA AS A MISSILE BASE BY THE SOVIET UNION
AND
LETTER FROM NORBERT A. SCHLEI TO
THE AUTHOR

MEMORANDUM FOR THE
ATTORNEY GENERAL

RE: LEGALITY UNDER INTERNATIONAL LAW
OF REMEDIAL ACTION AGAINST USE OF
CUBA AS A MISSILE BASE BY THE SOVIET UNION

This is in response to your request for the views of this Office as to certain legal issues bearing upon a proposed declaration by the President of the intentions of this Government in the event that missile bases should be established in Cuba by the Soviet Union. In general, it is our view that international law would permit use by the United States of relatively extreme measures, including various forms and degrees of force, for the purpose of terminating or preventing the realization of such a threat to the peace and security of the Western Hemisphere. An obligation would exist to have recourse first, if time should permit, to the procedures of collective security organizations of which the United States is a member. The United States would, further, be obliged to confine any use of force to the least necessary to the end proposed.

Section I of this Memorandum deals with the function and content of the concept of self-defense in international law generally. The next succeeding section examines certain regional differences which have developed in the application of that concept as a result of historical attitudes and practices and other factors. The Memorandum concludes with several concrete suggestions as to the form and content of the proposed statement by the President.

I

International law relating to the use of force centers about the polar concepts of aggression and self-defense. Although forcible violation of a state's boundaries or of its rights on the high seas is condemned by international law, the condemnation extends only to aggressive force. Even the most highly developed systems of municipal law permit the use of force in self-defense within relatively narrow limits. In the international community, where there exists no centralized authority capable of maintaining order, states must have, and are accorded by law, a proportionately greater freedom to protect their vital interests by unilateral action. Not only customary international law but the United Nations Charter and substantially all other conventions and treaties which relate to this subject recognize the indispensable role of self-defense under present conditions.

The concept of self-defense in international law of course justifies more than activity designed merely to resist an armed attack which is already in progress. Under international law every state has, in the words of Elihu Root, "the right . . . to protect itself by preventing a condition of affairs in which it will be too late to protect itself."[1] Cases commonly cited as illustrative of this principle include that of the *Virginius*,[2] in which Spanish forces seized an American vessel on the high seas en route to Cuba carrying arms for the use of insurgents. Britain demanded reparations for arbitrary treatment of its subjects found on board the vessel after the seizure was affected, but conceded the legality of the seizure itself. The United States withdrew its initial protest and eventually adopted the British view of the incident as its own. Similarly, in the case of the *Caroline*,[3] Canadian forces invaded the United States and destroyed the vessel, which was to be used by Canadian insurgents and American sympathizers in an attack on Canada. Many other illustrations of the principle could be cited.[4]

Although it is clear that the principle of self-defense may justify preventive action in foreign territory and on the high seas under some circumstances, it is also clear that this principle is subject to certain limitations. For example, such defensive action is subject to a rule of proportionality. Thus in the *Caroline* case the United States called upon Great Britain not only to justify the taking of preventive action, but also to show that its forces "did nothing unreasonable or excessive, since the act, justified by the necessity of self-defence, must be limited by that necessity and kept clearly within it."[5]

A further limitation on preventive action, at least unilateral action not sanctioned by any collective security arrangement, relates to the degree of urgency that must exist before it is invoked. In the next section of this Memorandum it is argued that, under the special regime applicable to the Western Hemisphere, the mere maintenance of facilities for certain kinds of armed attack, without more, may justify preventive action. However, apart from such special regimes, it is clear that preventive action in self-defense is warranted only where the need for it is "instant, overwhelming, leaving no choice of means, and no moment for deliberation."[6] It thus is clear that preventive action would not ordinarily be lawful to prevent the maintenance of missile bases or other

---

[1] *The Real Monroe Doctrine*, 35 A.J.I.L. 427, 432 (1914).

[2] 2 Moore, Digest of International Law 895–903, 980–983 (1906).

[3] Hall, International Law 328–330 (8th ed., Higgins, 1924); 1 Hyde, International Law 566 (2d ed. 1945).

[4] See, *e.g.*, Bowett, Self-Defence in International Law (1958), *passim*.

[5] Note of Mr. Webster, Secretary of State, to Lord Ashburton, July 28, 1842, Brit. and For. State Papers, Vol. XXX, p. 193.

[6] *Ibid.* Mr. Webster's statement was quoted with approval by the International Military Tribunal at Nuremberg. 41 A.J.I.L. 205 (1947).

armaments in the absence of evidence that their actual use for an aggressive attack was imminent.

Another limitation upon the concept of self-defense, as derived from customary law, is imposed by the United Nations Charter and the charters of regional collective security organizations, such as the Organization of American States, of which the United States is a member. The charters of these organizations in each case preserve the right of individual states to use force in self-defense, and, although certain ambiguities are presented by the language used, it appears that none of the charters prohibits the taking of unilateral preventive action in self defense prior to the occurrence of an armed attack. However, although it is arguable that there is no express commitment in these charters to utilize the procedures they afford in situations calling for preventive action, adherence to such an organization undoubtedly carries with it a commitment to have recourse to the organization's procedures if at all possible before acting unilaterally.[7] Indeed, an obligation to this effect might well be deduced from the general rules as to preventive action, summarized above, to the effect that such action is lawful only as a last resort. In any event, the United States is heavily committed to the use of collective security procedures as a matter of policy.

A further principle recognized in the U.N. Charter (Article 51) is that action may be taken in self-defense, pursuant to a regional collective security arrangement, by a state which is not directly threatened. If a sufficient threat against any member state is established, the organization and all its member may act. In this respect, the Charter has the effect of expanding the area in which preventive action is regarded as lawful.

Both the U.N. Charter and the Charter of the O.A.S. authorize collective action upon less provocation than would be required to justify unilateral action. The Security Council may take action against any "threat to the peace" or "breach of the peace" as well as any "act of aggression" (Article 39). Such action may include not only the economic and political sanctions listed in Article 41 but also "demonstrations, blockade, and other operations by air, sea, or land forces," as provided in Article 42. Action proposed in the Security Council is, of course, subject to veto by any one of the five permanent members. Upon a less explicit legal basis, the General Assembly may take similar action under the "Uniting-for-Peace" resolution. Under Article 25 of the Charter of the O.A.S. and Article 5 of the Rio Treaty, which are interrelated, measures

[7] Article 51 of the U.N. Charter requires that action taken in the exercise of the right of self-defense be reported to the Security Council. Unilateral action such as a blockade or an armed attack could, further, be brought before the O.A.S. for review by any member nation. Decisions by two-thirds vote of the Organ of Consultation created by the Rio Pact are binding upon all member states (Article 20), except that no state can be required to use armed force without its consent.

for the common defense may be taken not only in the event of an armed
attack but also if the "territory or sovereignty or political independence
of any American State" is affected by "an aggression which is not an
armed attack" or by "any other fact or situation that might endanger
the peace of America . . . ." Under Article 17 of the Rio Treaty, enforcement action requires a two-thirds vote in the Organ of Consultation.

II

Since the Monroe Doctrine was announced in 1823, the United States
has consistently maintained that it has the right to take all necessary
action to prevent any non-American power from obtaining control over
territory in the Western Hemisphere. Since 1846, when the so-called
Polk Corollary of the Doctrine was added, it has been understood that
this right is claimed regardless of whether the foreign intervention occurs
with the consent of inhabitants of the area affected. In modern times, it
has been understood that the right is claimed not only on behalf of the
United States but on behalf of all American states. The right has repeatedly been respected and acknowledged throughout the Americas
and the world.

Historical materials with respect to the Monroe Doctrine are collected in the Appendix which is attached. Perhaps the most relevant of
these materials are those relating to action taken by the United States
and other states in the Western Hemisphere during the period of 1940–41,
prior to their involvement in World War II. In 1940, by the Act of
Havana, the American powers agreed to prevent by collective action, or
by unilateral action if necessary, changes in the control of territory in the
Western Hemisphere as a result of the European hostilities. In 1941, the
United States occupied Greenland and dispatched troops to Iceland.
Although the occupation of Greenland was justified in part under a
treaty with the Danish government in exile, it seems clear that the true
basis for the action taken by the United States was the concept of
regional self-defense expressed in the Monroe Doctrine.[8]

The historical materials which are appended show that the Monroe
Doctrine has from the beginning represented a regional variation in the
international law of self-defense. The Doctrine asserts that, in order to
insulate the Americas from dangers to peace and security stemming
from conflicts involving non-American states, the occupation or control
of American territory by a non-American power in itself shall be deemed
to present a sufficient danger to warrant exercise by the United States
and other American powers of the right of self-defense. The result of the
consistent adherence to this attitude by the United States and most other
American states, together with the acquiescence of the rest of the civil-

[8] See, e.g., Briggs, 35 A.J.I.L. 506 (1941).

ized world, has been to create a specialized, regional body of law under which preventive action in self-defense is, in the Americas, authorized under less restrictive conditions than would be required in some other regions.

In more recent years, the United States has ceased to maintain the Monroe Doctrine in the more extreme forms which it assumed in the late nineteenth and early twentieth centuries. The Doctrine today does not protect purely economic or political interests, as it once did, or even security interests which are less than fundamental. Thus the United States has refrained from direct intervention in Cuba to prevent the mere continuance in office, apart from any specific military threat, of a government which is allied with the Communist Bloc and which has not hesitated to destroy economic interests of the United States in the island. The United States has further refrained from forcible intervention to prevent shipment of conventional arms to Cuba, thus tolerating a certain degree of danger that such arms might be used for aggressive purposes against the United States or against other American nations. So far the United States has withheld action in deference to conceptions, entertained strongly in some quarters in Latin America, of self-determination and non-intervention. However, thus far it has been arguable that under modern conditions, no critical danger to the peace and security of other countries in the Western Hemisphere was presented; that shipments of conventional arms to the Castro Government could not necessarily be ascribed to any purpose beyond the defense of Cuba. The same cannot be said of missiles, certainly not of ground-to-ground missiles. The use of Cuban territory to mount such weapons, usable by the Soviet Union only to attack other states and not merely for the defense of Cuba against attack, falls wholly outside the reasons for mitigation by the United States of some aspects of the Monroe Doctrine. Equally important, it falls wholly outside the reasons advanced by our allies in Latin America for opposing interventionist aspects of the Doctrine.

There is nothing unique about the concept of regional differences, based upon historical attitudes and practices, in the impact and requirements of international law. In the *Anglo-Norwegian Fisheries Case*,[9] for example, the International Court of Justice upheld a system for determining the baselines and boundaries of Norway's territorial sea that could be valid outside Norway, if at all, only in the Scandinavian region. In so doing, the Court relied upon "interests peculiar to [the] region, the reality and importance of which are clearly evidenced by a long usage," and upon the "general toleration of foreign states" over an extended period.[10] Regional variations are also familiar features of the law of the sea with respect to bays and with respect to sedentary fisheries.

[9] Judgment of Dec. 18, 1951, [1951] I.C.J. Rep. 116.
[10] *Id.*, pp. 133, 138.

In a Memorandum for the Attorney General dated April 12, 1961, Assistant Attorney General Katzenbach noted that traditional legal doctrines relating to intervention date from the pre-World War I period and reflect the existence at that time of a security structure based upon flexibility of alignment. Since change of alignment to preserve a balance of power was the principal technique by which security was maintained, legal doctrines tended to develop that would promote freedom to change alignment and would discourage intervention for the purpose of maintaining existing alignments.

The Memorandum continues as follows:

"The political structure today is vastly different. Alignments within the Communist Bloc and within the West are long-term political alignments with considerable aspects of supra-national authority. As a result, the security system from the point of view of each bloc depends less upon neutrality of alignment than it does upon preserving the alignments which exist. Therefore, . . . there is considerable pressure for intervention in situations where bloc security is threatened. There is nothing in the existing legal structure which recognizes this state of affairs, but there are numerous instances where intervention has been tolerated in the postwar period; for example, Hungary, Guatemala, Lebanon, and, in 1948, Israel."

Although it is true that traditional legal concepts of general application do not expressly recognize interests in bloc security, the Monroe Doctrine constitutes an explicit qualification on a regional basis of general legal concepts insofar as the Western Hemisphere is concerned. The history of the Doctrine includes many incidents which emphasize its purpose to prohibit flatly the adherence of territories in the Americas to European or Asiatic power blocs, or for that matter the transfer by them of allegiance from one bloc to another.[11] The premise underlying this purpose—that peace and security in the Hemisphere could be assured only by insulating it from the unstable alliances and rivalries of Europe and Asia—squarely contradicts the balance-of-power policies that infuse the doctrines of general application which are altered by the Doctrine.

Moreover, although publicists in the field of international law have not yet formulated concepts and doctrines which expressly recognize the changed world situation, it seems probable that international law as reflected in the actual practices and expectations of states, already recognizes the decisive importance of bloc security today in certain geographic areas. International law is, after all, essentially a generalized statement in terms of rules and policies of the reasonable expectations of states as derived from their practices in making claims and reacting to the claims of others. The western states have, of course, condemned as

[11] See generally Logan, No Transfer—An American Security Principle (1961).

unlawful the Soviet intervention in Hungary, directed as it was against a revolt which at the time posed a purely political threat against the Soviet Union. It may be doubted, however, whether the United States would have protested seriously the use of force by the Soviet Union if it had been designed for the limited purpose of compelling abandonment of a plan to install Western missile bases in Hungarian territory.

If in the future the government of Poland should become increasingly friendly to the United States, our government would undoubtedly defend strongly its legal right to withdraw from the Communist political bloc. It seems altogether certain that we would, however, feel obliged to refrain from attempting to supply Poland with ground-to-ground missiles or other armaments readily susceptible of aggressive use. Yugoslavia, and perhaps Finland as well, provide examples of states which the international community as a whole probably regards as insulated, under threat of intervention by the Soviet Union, from full incorporation into the western military structure.

In appraising the rights of the United States vis-a-vis Cuba, the treaty of 1934 [12] may have some relevance. The principal effect of the treaty was to abrogate the Cuban–American Treaty of 1903,[13] under which the United States had the right to intervene in Cuba virtually at will. However, the treaty of 1934 preserved existing agreements indefinitely with respect to the leasing of naval stations in Cuba insofar as they applied to the naval station at Guantanamo. The Treaty of 1934 did not expressly obligate Cuba to refrain from permitting the use of its territory for military purposes by other states. However, the fair inference arising from the cession of naval rights to the United States is that the island was to be a part of, or at least not a breach in, the defensive military system protecting the continental United States and the Caribbean countries. At the time of the treaty, of course, a military threat to these areas from Cuba could arise only as a consequence of naval and air installations of the type which the treaty secured to the United States. The evident intention of the parties to the treaty, broadly stated, thus was to restrict intervention by the United States on political or economic grounds, but to preserve the position of Cuba in the defensive military system of the United States. Certainly the treaty is not inconsistent with the position here expressed as to the legal rights of the United States in the event of military use of Cuban territory by the Soviet Union.

It should be apparent that the conclusions here reached do not undermine the legal position of the United States with respect to its own missile bases abroad. In no case of which we are aware is a country in which the United States maintains missile bases subject to a special regime comparable to the Monroe Doctrine. Moreover, in no case is any such country a member or former member of the Communist Bloc or within

[12] State Dep't, Treaty Information Bulletin No. 56 (1934).
[13] Foreign Relations of the United States (1904) 243–246.

the acknowledged periphery of the Soviet security system. Finally, there is a basic factual difference in the military relationships of such countries to the Soviet Union and that of Cuba to the United States. The States in which bases are maintained by the United States are in each case among the major targets of Soviet military preparations. No impartial observer could conclude that Cuba is a major object of the military program of the United States, or that Cuba is in any danger of a missile attack by the United States. The United Kingdom may harbor U.S. missiles in self-defense because it is a likely target of Soviet missiles. For Cuba to harbor Soviet missiles would constitute a wholly disproportionate response to any sane estimate of its defensive needs against the United States.

III

We assume that any statement by the President on this subject would begin by announcing that there is reason to believe the governments of Cuba and the Soviet Union may be actively considering the installation of Soviet missiles on Cuban territory, and would be designed generally to warn those countries of the intentions of the United States in any such eventuality. We offer the following suggestions with regard to such a statement by the President:

(1) The statement should emphasize the historical and regional aspects of the rights being asserted by the United States.

(2) The statement should emphasize the threat to other countries as well as the United States, and the defensive character of any action that might be taken by the United States. Possibly the statement should expressly disclaim any intention to act for economic or political ends, or for any purpose other than to compel an abandonment of plans to create a specific military threat in Cuba.

(3) The statement should indicate an intention to have recourse first, if at all possible, to collective security arrangements to which the United States is a party, particularly the Organization of American States. It should also, without qualifying the strong commitment of the United States to the principle of collective security, make the point that the United States has an ultimate responsibility for its own safety which in situations of extreme gravity necessarily would take precedence over all other commitments. Consideration should be given to withholding the statement until it can be made as a first step in an integrated plan to secure collective action by the O.A.S. If made in that context, the statement should announce a call for a meeting of the Organ of Consultation pursuant to the Inter-American Treaty of Reciprocal Assistance (Rio Pact).

(4) The statement should acknowledge an obligation on the part of the United States to observe a rule of proportionality. An express

reference might be made to total blockade or to "visit and search" procedures as appropriate reactions by the American states or by the United States to meet a threat to install missile bases in Cuba. In this connection, care should certainly be exercised to avoid the implication that Cuba is under any immediate threat of nuclear attack.

Norbert A. Schlei
Assistant Attorney General
Office of Legal Counsel

APPENDIX HISTORICAL MATERIAL WITH RESPECT TO THE MONROE DOCTRINE

1. *The Monroe Doctrine—1823*

The Monroe Doctrine was proclaimed by President Monroe in his message to Congress on December 9, 1923. This proclamation of fundamental principles of American foreign policy in the Western Hemisphere was induced by several factors—the intervention of the three leading absolute monarchies of Russia, Austria, and Prussia (the so-called "Holy Alliance") in the affairs of other European countries, the fear that they might attempt to overthrow the newly independent Latin-American states and restore them as Spanish colonies, and Russian claims in the Western Hemisphere.[1] President Monroe's message stated in part:[2]

"The occasion has been judged proper for asserting as a principle in which the rights and interests of the United States are involved, that the American continents, by the free and independent condition which they have assumed and maintain, are henceforth not to be considered as subjects for future colonization by any European powers. . . . The political system of the allied powers is essentially different in this respect from that of America. . . . We owe it, therefore, to candor, and to the amicable relations existing between the United States and those powers, to declare that we should consider any attempt on their part to extend their system to any portion of this hemisphere as dangerous to our peace and safety. With the existing colonies or dependencies of

[1] Alverez, *The Monroe Doctrine*, 6–7 (1924).
[2] J. D. Richardson, *A Compilation of the Messages and Papers of the Presidents, 1789–1897*, vol. II, pp. 209, 218, 219.

any European power we have not interfered and shall not interfere. But with the Governments who have declared their independence, and maintained it, and whose independence we have, on great consideration and on just principles, acknowledged, we could not view any interposition for the purpose of oppressing them, or controlling in any other manner their destiny, by any European power, in any other light than as the manifestation of an unfriendly disposition towards the United States. . . . It is impossible that the allied powers should extend their political system to any portion of either [American] continent without endangering our peace and happiness; nor can anyone believe that our southern brethren, if left to themselves, would adopt it of their own accord. It is equally impossible, therefore, that we should behold such interposition, in any form, with indifference."

2. The Polk Corollary—1848

In 1848 Mexican officials in Yucatan indicated a willingness to permit annexation of territory under their jurisdiction by Great Britain or Spain in return for protection against the rebellious native Indian population. To forestall any possibility of European intervention in Mexico, President Polk sent a special message to Congress on April 29, 1848, enunciating what is known as the Polk Corollary of the Monroe Doctrine. The President's message declared in part:[3]

"I submit for the consideration of Congress several communications received at the Department of State from Mr. Justo Sierra, commissioner of Yucatan, and also a communication from the Governor of that State, representing the condition of extreme suffering to which their country has been reduced by an insurrection of the Indians within its limits, and asking the aid of the United States.

*   *   *

"In this condition they have, through their constituted authorities, implored the aid of this Government to save them from destruction, offering in case this should be granted to transfer the 'dominion and sovereignty of the peninsula' to the United States. Similar appeals for aid and protection have been made to the Spanish and the English Governments.

"Whilst it is not my purpose to recommend the adoption of any measure with a view to the acquisition of the 'dominion and sovereignty' over Yucatan, yet, according to our established policy, we could not consent to a transfer of this 'dominion and sovereignty' either to Spain, Great Britain, or any other European power. In the language of President Monroe in his message of December, 1823—

[3] Id., vol. 4, pp. 581–582.

'We should consider any attempt on their part to extend their system to any portion of this hemisphere as dangerous to our peace and safety.'

*   *   *

"Our own security requires that the established policy thus announced should guide our conduct, and this applies with great force to the peninsula of Yucatan. It is situate in the Gulf of Mexico, on the North American continent, and, from its vicinity to Cuba, to the capes of Florida, to New Orleans, and, indeed, to our whole southwestern coast, it would be dangerous to our peace and security if it should become a colony of any European nation."

3. *President Johnson and European Intervention in Mexico—1865–1866*

In 1861 and 1862, during the Civil War, France, Great Britain and Spain invaded Mexico. After the British and Spanish withdrew, Emperor Napoleon III of France selected Archduke Maximilian of Austria as Emperor of Mexico. Maximilian accepted on the basis of "proof" given by Napoleon and by Mexican exiles in France that the Mexican people wanted him. Because of its involvement in the Civil War, the United States could not interfere. After the war, Secretary of State Seward reaffirmed the principles of the Monroe Doctrine, although he did not refer to it by name.[4] The House of Representatives then adopted a resolution declaring that—

". . . it does not accord with the policy of the United States to acknowledge any monarchical government erected on the ruins of any republican government in America under the auspices of any European power."[5]

In his First Annual Message to Congress on December 4, 1865, President Johnson said in this connection:[6]

"From the moment of the establishment of our free Constitution the civilized world has been convulsed by revolutions in the interests of democracy or of monarchy, but through all those revolutions the United States have wisely and firmly refused to become propagandists of republicanism. It is the only government suited to our condition; but we have never sought to impose it on others, and we have consistently followed the advice of Washington to recommend it only by the careful preservation and prudent use of the blessing. . . . Twice, indeed, rumours of the invasion of some parts of America in the in-

---

[4] Pratt, *A History of the United States Foreign Policy, 342* (1955).
[5] *Id.*
[6] Richardson, *op. cit.*, vol. 6, pp. 353, 368–369.

terest of monarchy have prevailed; twice my predecessors have had occasion to announce the views of this nation in respect to such interference. On both occasions the remonstrance of the United States was respected from a deep conviction on the part of European Governments that the system of noninterference and mutual abstinence from propagandism was the true rule for the two hemispheres. . . . We should regard it as a great calamity to ourselves, to the cause of good government, and to the peace of the world should any European power challenge the American people, as it were, to the defense of republicanism against foreign interference. We can not foresee and are unwilling to consider what opportunities might present themselves, what combinations might offer to protect ourselves against designs inimical to our form of government. The United States desire to act in the future as they have ever acted heretofore; they never will be driven from that course but by the aggression of European powers, and we rely on the wisdom and justice of those powers to respect the system of noninterference which has so long been sanctioned by time, and which by its good results has approved itself to both continents.'

Finally, in 1866, the French Government withdrew its forces from Mexico and the Mexicans overthrew the Maximilian regime in 1867.

4. *President Hayes and the Isthmian Canal Question—1880*

In 1879 it appeared imminent that a private French company was about to undertake the construction of a canal across the Panama Isthmus. The United States feared that control of the canal would fall into the hands of the French Government just as the British Government had earlier obtained control of the Suez Canal. On March 8, 1880, President Hayes sent a message to Congress expressing his opposition to the project as follows:

"The United States can not consent to the surrender of this control to any European power or to any combination of European powers. If existing treaties between the United States and other nations or if the rights of sovereignty or property of other nations stand in the way of this policy—a contingency which is not apprehended—suitable steps should be taken by just and liberal negotiations to promote and establish the American policy on this subject consistently with the rights of the nations to be affected by it.

"The capital invested by corporations or citizens of other countries in such an enterprise must in a great degree look for protection to one or more of the great powers of the world. No European power can intervene for such protection without adopting measures on this

⁷ *Id.* vol. 7, pp. 585–586.

continent which the United States would deem wholly inadmissible. If the protection of the United States is relied upon, the United States must exercise such control as will enable this country to protect its national interests and maintain the rights of those whose private capital is embarked in the work.

"An interoceanic canal across the American Isthmus will essentially change the geographical relations between the Atlantic and Pacific coasts of the United States and between the United States and the rest of the world. It would be the great ocean thoroughfare between our Atlantic and our Pacific shores, and virtually a part of the coast line of the United States. Our merely commercial interest in it is greater than that of all other countries, while its relations to our power and prosperity as a nation, to our means of defence, our unity, peace, and safety, are matters of paramount concern to the people of the United States. No other great power would under similar circumstances fail to assert a rightful control over a work so closely and vitally affecting its interest and welfare.

"Without urging further the grounds of my opinion, I repeat, in conclusion, that it is the right and the duty of the United States to assert and maintain such supervision and authority over any interoceanic canal across the isthmus that connects North and South America as will protect our national interests. This, I am quite sure, will be found not only compatible with but promotive of the widest and most permanent advantage to commerce and civilization."

In addition, both Houses of Congress formally protested against any canal which might be built by foreign capital or controlled by foreign nations.[8]

5. *President Cleveland's Intervention in the Venezuela Boundary Dispute—1895*

In President Cleveland's second administration, he invoked the Monroe Doctrine in the British–Venezuela dispute concerning the boundaries between British Guiana and Venezuela. The British being unwilling to arbitrate the matter, the President in a special message to Congress on December 17, 1895, announced that under the principles of the Monroe Doctrine the United States would designate a commission which would itself investigate the boundary and render a report.[9] In the event the report favored Venezuela in the dispute, he said, "it will, in my opinion, be the duty of the United States to resist by every means in its power as a willful aggression upon its rights and interests, the appropriation by Great Britain of any lands or the exercise of governmental jurisdiction over any territory which after investigation we have determined of right belongs to Venezuela. In making these recommendations

[8] Bailey, *A Diplomatic History of the American People*, 396–397 (1955).
[9] Richardson, vol. 9, *op. cit. supra*, p. 655, 658.

I am fully alive to the responsibility incurred and keenly realize all the consequences that may follow." [10] He further said: [11]

". . . it may not be amiss to suggest that the doctrine upon which we stand is strong and sound, because its enforcement is important to our peace and safety as a nation and is essential to the integrity of our free institutions and the tranquil maintenance of our distinctive form of government. It was intended to apply to every stage of our national life and can not become obsolete while our Republic endures. If the balance of power is justly a cause for jealous anxiety among the Governments of the Old World and a subject for our absolute no-interference, none the less is an observance of the Monroe doctrine of vital concern to our people and their Government.

"Assuming, therefore, that we may properly insist upon this doctrine without regard to 'the state of things in which we live' or any changed conditions here or elsewhere, it is not apparent why its application may not be invoked in the present controversy.

"If a European power by an extension of its boundaries takes possession of the territory of one of our neighbouring Republics against its will and in derogation of its rights, it is difficult to see why to that extent such European power does not thereby attempt to extend its system of government to that portion of this continent which is thus taken. This is the precise action which President Monroe declared to be 'dangerous to our peace and safety,' and it can make no difference whether the European system is extended by an advance of frontier or otherwise."

Addressing himself to the contention that the Monroe Doctrine found no support in any principle of international law derived from the general consent of nations, the President stated: [12]

"Practically the principle for which we contend has peculiar, if not exclusive, relation to the United States. It may not have been admitted in so many words to the code of international law, but since in international councils every nation is entitled to the rights belonging to it, if the enforcement of the Monroe doctrine is something we may justly claim it has its place in the code of international law as certainly and as securely as if it were specifically mentioned; and when the United States is a suitor before the high tribunal that administers international law the question to be determined is whether or not we present claims which the justice of that code of law can find to be right and valid.

"The Monroe doctrine finds its recognition in those principles of international law which are based upon the theory that every nation shall have its rights protected and its just claims enforced."

[10] *Id.*, 688.   [11] *Id.*, 656.   [12] *Id.*, 656–657.

The British Prime Minister acknowledged that the interests of the United States in the Caribbean area were as natural as British concern would be over any attempt by a great European power to secure control over the Channel ports of Belgium and the Netherlands. The British finally submitted the controversy to arbitration.[13]

6. Cuba—The Platt Amendment—President Theodore Roosevelt—1901

Congress, on March 1, 1901, passed the Platt Amendment to the Army Appropriation bill. The amendment defined the relations between Cuba and the United States following the establishment of the Cuban republic. It provided that in order to permit the United States to maintain Cuba's independence, and to protect its people, Cuba would sell or lease to the United States lands necessary for coaling or naval stations at certain specified points, to be agreed upon with the President of the United States; and that Cuba would embody the foregoing provisions in a permanent treaty with the United States. 31 Stat. 897–898. The amendment in effect contemplated a United States quasi-protectorate over Cuba. Later that year Cuba incorporated these provisions as an appendix to its constitution. Foreign Relations of the United States, 244 (1904).

In his message to Congress on December 3, 1901, President Theodore Roosevelt discussed the Monroe Doctrine in relation to Cuba. The President said:[14]

"The Monroe Doctrine should be the cardinal feature of the foreign policy of all the nations of the two Americas, as it is of the United States. Just seventy-eight years have passed since President Monroe in his Annual Message announced that 'The American continents are henceforth not to be considered as subjects for future colonization by any European power.' In other words, the Monroe Doctrine is a declaration that there must be no territorial aggrandizement by any non-American power at the expense of any American power on American soil. It is in no wise intended as hostile to any nation in the Old World. Still less is it intended to give cover to any aggression by one New World power at the expense of any other. It is simply a step, and a long step, toward assuring the universal peace of the world by securing the possibility of permanent peace on this hemisphere.

"During the past century other influences have established the permanence and independence of the smaller states of Europe. Through the Monroe Doctrine we hope to be able to safeguard like independence and secure like permanence for the lesser among the New World nations.

*   *   *

---

[13] Sears, History of American Foreign Relations, 431 (1938).
[14] Richardson, op. cit., supra, (Supp. by Devitt. 1897–1902) 338–339.

"Our attitude in Cuba is a sufficient guaranty of our own good faith. We have not the slightest desire to secure any territory at the expense of any of our neighbours. We wish to work with them hand in hand, so that all of us may be uplifted together, and we rejoice over the good fortune of any of them, we gladly hail their material prosperity and political stability, and are concerned and alarmed if any of them fall into industrial or political chaos. We do not wish to see any Old World military power grow up on this continent, or to be compelled to become a military power ourselves. The peoples of the Americas can prosper best if left to work out their own salvation in their own way."

In the Cuban–American treaty of 1903,[15] Cuba agreed not to enter into any treaty or other compact with a foreign power which would impair its independence or permit military or naval control by a foreign power. It also agreed that the United States should have the right to intervene to preserve Cuban independence. The United States, for its defense as well as that of Cuba, was to have the right to maintain naval bases in Cuba. Pursuant to the treaty, a permanent naval base was established at Guantanamo.[16]

In 1905 the President addressed a message to Congress, stating:[17]

"One of the most effective instruments for peace is the Monroe Doctrine as it has been and is being gradually developed by this Nation and accepted by other nations. No other policy could have been as efficient in promoting peace in the Western Hemisphere and in giving to each nation thereon the chance to develop along its own lines. If we had refused to apply the doctrine to changing conditions it would now be completely outworn, would not meet any of the needs of the present day, and, indeed, would probably by this time have sunk into complete oblivion. It is useful at home, and is meeting with recognition abroad because we have adapted our application of it to meet the growing and changing needs of the hemisphere. When we announce a policy such as the Monroe Doctrine we thereby commit ourselves to the consequences of the policy, and those consequences from time to time alter. It is out of the question to claim a right and yet shirk the responsibility for its exercise. Not only we, but all American republics who are benefited by the existence of the doctrine, must recognize the obligations each nation is under as regards foreign peoples no less than its duty to insist upon its own rights.

"That our rights and interests are deeply concerned in the main-

---

[15] 33 Stat. 2248–2253.
[16] Foreign Relations of the United States, 350–353 (1903).
[17] Richardson (Supp. by Lewis, 1901–1905) *op. cit.*, *supra* 1178–1181.

tenance of the doctrine is so clear as hardly to need argument. This is especially true in view of the construction of the Panama Canal. As a mere matter of self-defense we must exercise a close watch over the approaches to this canal; and this means that we must be thoroughly alive to our interests in the Caribbean Sea.

"There are certain essential points which must never be forgotten as regards the Monroe Doctrine. In the first place we must as a Nation make it evident that we do not intend to treat it in any shape or way as an excuse for aggrandizement on our part at the expense of the republics to the south. We must recognize the fact that in some South American countries there has been much suspicion lest we should interpret the Monroe Doctrine as in some way inimical to their interests, and we must try to convince all the other nations of this continent once and for all that no just and orderly Government has anything to fear from us. . . . It must be understood that under no circumstances will the United States use the Monroe Doctrine as a cloak for territorial aggression. We desire peace with all the world, but perhaps most of all with the other people of the American Continent. . . .

7. Elihu Root on the Monroe Doctrine—1914

Elihu Root was President Roosevelt's Secretary of State from 1905–1909. Subsequently Root became President of the American Society of International Law. In his exposition in 1914 in the American Journal of International Law of the Monroe Doctrine, he said:[18]

"No one ever pretended that Mr. Monroe was declaring a rule of international law or that the doctrine which he declared has become international law. It is a declaration of the United States that certain acts would be injurious to the peace and safety of the United States and that the United States would regard them as unfriendly. The declaration does not say what the course of the United States will be in case such acts are done. That is left to be determined in each particular instance.

*   *   *

"The doctrine is not international law but it rests upon the right of self-protection and that right is recognized by international law. The right is a necessary corollary of independent sovereignty. It is well understood that the exercise of the right of self-protection may and frequently does extend in its effect beyond the limits of the territorial jurisdiction of the state exercising it. The strongest example probably would be the mobilization of an army by another Power immediately across the frontier. Every act done by the other Power may be within

[18] Root, *The Real Monroe Doctrine*, 8 Am. J. Int. L. 427, 431–432 (1914).

its own territory. Yet the country threatened by the state of facts is justified in protecting itself by immediate war. The most common exercise of the right of self-protection outside of a state's own territory and in time of peace is the interposition of objection to the occupation of territory, of points of strategic military or maritime advantage, or to indirect accomplishment of this effect by dynastic arrangement. For example, the objection of England in 1911 to the occupation of a naval station by Germany on the Atlantic coast of Morocco; the objection of the European Powers generally to the vast force of Russia extending its territory to the Mediterranean; the revision of the Treaty of San Stefano by the Treaty of Berlin; the establishment of buffer states; the objection to the succession of a German prince to the throne of Spain; the many forms of the eastern question; the centuries of struggle to preserve the balance of power in Europe; all depend upon the very same principle which underlies the Monroe Doctrine; that is to say, upon *the right of every sovereign state to protect itself by preventing a condition of affairs in which it will be too late to protect itself.* Of course each state must judge for itself when a threatened act will create such a situation. If any state objects to a threatened act and the reasonableness of its objection is not assented to, the efficacy of the objection will depend upon the power behind it. (*Italics* added).

8. *The Magdalena Bay Episode—1912*

In 1912 it was asserted that a Japanese private fishing company was about to lease from the Government of Mexico an extensive tract of land on the shore of Magdalena Bay, in Lower California, Mexico. This land could be used as the site of a naval base capable of intercepting communications between the Pacific coast of the United States and the Panama Canal. The Senate, adopted a resolution proposed by Senator Lodge as follows:[19]

"Resolved, That when any harbor or other place in the American continents is so situated that the occupation thereof for naval or military purposes might threaten the communications or the safety of the United States, the Government of the United States could not see without grave concern the possession of such harbor or other place by any corporation or association which has such a relation to another Government, not American, as to give that Government practical power of control for naval or military purposes."

9. *President Wilson and Vera Cruz—1914*

In 1914 President Wilson was notified that a German merchantman was approaching Vera Cruz, Mexico, with a large cargo of arms which

[19] Cong. Record, 62 Cong. 2d Sess., pp. 10045–10046.

it was suspected the Huerto Government intended to use against the United States. The President ordered American forces to seize the port; a battle ensued, and the objective of preventing the arms from reaching Huerto's forces was attained.[20] American forces then occupied the city, and a proclamation was issued prohibiting the importation of arms into Mexico.

This armed intervention terminated diplomatic relations between the United States and Mexico. However, Argentina, Brazil and Chile offered to mediate the controversy and President Wilson accepted.

10. *Charles Evans Hughes and the Monroe Doctrine—1923*

Mr. Hughes, Secretary of State in the Harding Administration, delivered an address in 1923 on the Monroe Doctrine before the American Bar Association which is often cited as an authoritative statement He said:[21]

"It is not my purpose to review the historical applications of what is called the Monroe doctrine or to attempt to harmonize the various redactions of it. Properly understood, it is opposed (1) to any non-American action encroaching upon the political independence of American States under any guise and (2) to the acquisition in any manner of the control of additional territory in this hemisphere by any non-American power.

"The Monroe doctrine is not a legislative pronouncement; it has been approved by action of Congress, but it does not rest upon any congressional sanction. It has had the implied indorsement of the treaty-making power in the reservations to the two Hague conventions of 1899 and 1907, but it is not defined by treaty and does not draw its force from any international agreement. It is not like a constitutional provision deriving its authority from the fact that it is a part of the organic law transcending and limiting executive and legislative power. It is not a part of international law, maintained by the consent of the civilized powers and alterable only at their will. It is a policy declared by the Executive of the United States and repeated in one form and another by Presidents and Secretaries of State in the conduct of our foreign relations. Its significance lies in the fact that in its essentials, as set forth by President Monroe and as forcibly and repeatedly asserted by our responsible statesmen, it has been for 100 years, and continues to be, an integral part of our national thought and purpose, expressing a profound conviction which even the upheaval caused by the Great War, and our participation in that

---

[20] Bailey, *op. cit. supra*, pp. 558–560.
[21] Hughes, "Observations on the Monroe Doctrine," in Alvarez, *The Monroe Doctrine*, 413, 417–418 (1924).

struggle upon European soil, has not uprooted or fundamentally changed."

Mr. Hughes summarized the principles of the Doctrine as follows:

"First. The Monroe doctrine is not a policy of aggression; it is a policy of self-defense. It was asserted at a time when the danger of foreign aggression in this hemisphere was very real, when the new American States had not yet established a firm basis of independent national life, and we were menaced by threats of Old World powers directed against republican institutions. But the achievements of the century have not altered the scope of the doctrine or changed its basis. It still remains an assertion of the principle of national security. As such, it is obviously not exclusive. Much time has been wasted in the endeavor to find in the Monroe doctrine either justification, or the lack of it, for every governmental declaration or action in relation to other American States. Appropriate action for our defense may always be taken, and our proper influence to promote peace and good will may always be exerted, with the use of good offices to that end, whether or not the particular exigency comes within the range of the specific declarations which constitute the doctrine.[22]

*   *   *

"Second, As the policy embodied in the Monroe doctrine is distinctively the policy of the United States, the Government of the United States reserves to itself its definition, interpretation, and application. This Government has welcomed the recognition by other governments of the fact and soundness of this policy and of the appropriateness of its application from time to time. Great powers have signified their acquiescence in it. But the United States has not been disposed to enter into engagements which would have the effect of submitting to any other power or to any concert of powers the determination either of the occasions upon which the principles of the Monroe doctrine shall be invoked or of the measures that shall be taken in giving it effect. This Government has not been willing to make the doctrine or the regulation of its enforcement the subject of treaties with European powers; and, while the United States has been gratified at expressions on the part of other American States of their accord with our Government in its declarations with respect to their independence and at their determination to maintain it, this Government in asserting and pursuing its policy has commonly avoided concerted action to maintain the doctrine, even with the American Republics. As President Wilson observed: 'The Monroe doctrine was proclaimed by the United States on her own authority. It always has

[22] *Id.*, 418–419

been maintained and will always be maintained upon her own responsibility.' . . .[23]

"Third. The policy of the Monroe doctrine does not infringe upon the independence and sovereignty of other American States. Misconception upon this point is the only disturbing influence in our relations with Latin American States. . . .[24]

"This notion springs from a misunderstanding of the doctrine itself and of our national sentiment and purpose. . . .

"The Monroe doctrine does not attempt to establish a protectorate over Latin American States. . . .

"That ground [of the declaration] is found in the recognized right which every State enjoys, and the United States no less than any other, to object to acts done by other powers which threaten its own safety. The United States has all the rights of sovereignty, as well as any other power; we have lost none of our essential rights because we are strong, and other American States have gained none either because of increasing strength or relative weakness. . . .[25]

"Fourth. There are, indeed, modern conditions and recent events which can not fail to engage our attention. We have grown rich and powerful, but we have not outgrown the necessity, in justice to ourselves and without injustice to others, of safeguarding our future peace and security. . . .[26]

"Fifth. It is apparent that the Monroe doctrine does not stand in the way of Pan American cooperation; rather it affords the necessary foundation for that cooperation in the independence and security of American States."[27]

11. *The Clark Memorandum and President Hoover—1928*

In 1928 a *Memorandum on the Monroe Doctrine* was prepared by J. Reuben Clark, then Undersecretary of State, for use by the Secretary of State. It repudiated the (Theodore) "Roosevelt corollary" that "in case of financial or other difficulties in weak Latin American countries, the United States should attempt an adjustment thereof lest European Governments should intervene, and intervening should occupy territory."[28] Clark's thesis was that this was not "justified by the terms of the Monroe Doctrine, however much it may be justified by the application of self-preservation."[29] Clark's conclusions about the Doctrine were as follows:[30]

[23] *Id.*, 419–420.
[24] *Id.*, 421. [25] *Id.*, 422. [26] *Id.*, 424. [27] *Id.*, 431.
[28] Clark, *Memorandum on the Monroe Doctrine*, December 17, 1928, XXIII (pub. 1930).
[29] *Id.*, XXIII–XXIV.
[30] *Id.*, XXIV–XXV.

"The Doctrine does not concern itself with purely inter-American relations; it has nothing to do with the relationship between the United States and other American nations, except where other American nations shall become involved with European governments in arrangements which threaten the security of the United States, and even in such cases, the Doctrine runs against the European Country, not the American nation, and the United States would primarily deal thereunder with the European country and not with the American nation concerned. The Doctrine states a case of the United States *vs.* Europe, and not of the United States *vs.* Latin America. Furthermore, the fact should never be lost to view that in applying this Doctrine during the period of one hundred years since it was announced, our Government has over and over again driven it in as a shield between Europe and the Americas to protect Latin America from the political and territorial thrusts of Europe; and this was done at times when the American nations were weak and struggling for the establishment of stable, permanent governments; when the political morality of Europe sanctioned, indeed encouraged, the acquisition of territory by force; and when many of the great powers of Europe looked with eager, covetous eyes to the rich, undeveloped areas of the American hemisphere. Nor should another equally vital fact be lost sight of, that the United States has only been able to give this protection against designing European powers because of its known willingness and determination, if and whenever necessary, to expend its treasure and to sacrifice American life to maintain the principles of the Doctrine. So far as Latin America is concerned, the Doctrine is now, and always has been, not an instrument of violence and oppression, but an unbought, freely bestowed, and wholly effective guaranty of their freedom, independence, and territorial integrity against the imperialistic designs of Europe."

In embarking on a "Good Neighbor" policy, it has been said that President Hoover gave his support to the views expressed by Clark.[31]

12. *President Franklin D. Roosevelt—Abrogation of the Platt Amendment—the Inter-American Conference—Canada—1934-1938*

The Good Neighbor Policy was followed and implemented by President Franklin D. Roosevelt in an attempt to make the policy of nonintervention acceptable in both hemispheres. As an integral part of the new policy, the United States decided to release Cuba from the provisions of the Platt Amendment, *supra*. This was accomplished by a treaty between the United States and Cuba signed in May 1934.[32] Article III of

[31] Bailey, *op. cit. supra*, p. 681.
[32] State Department, Treaty Information Bulletin 56: May 1934.

this treaty, which continued the right of the United States to maintain a naval base at Guantanamo, provided as follows: [33]

> "Until the two contracting parties agree to the modification or abrogation of the stipulations of the agreement in regard to the lease to the United States of America of lands in Cuba for coaling and naval stations signed by the President of the Republic of Cuba on February 16, 1903, and by the President of the United States of America on the 23rd day of the same month and year, the stipulations of that agreement with regard to the naval station of Guantanamo shall continue in effect. The supplementary agreement in regard to naval or coaling stations signed between the two Governments on July 2, 1903, also shall continue in effect in the same form and on the same conditions with respect to the naval station at Guantanamo. So long as the United States of America shall not abandon the said naval station of Guantanamo or the two Governments shall not agree to a modification of its present limits, the station shall continue to have the territorial area that it now has, with the limits that it has on the date of the signature of the present Treaty."

In 1936 President Roosevelt proposed a special InterAmerican peace conference. At this conference, held at Buenos Aires, he invited all American states to resort to the principles of the Monroe Doctrine in dealing with aggressive threats by non-American totalitarian states and declared that such states seeking "to commit Acts of aggression against us will find a hemisphere wholly prepared to consult together for our mutual safety and our mutual good." [34]

In 1938, Canada supported President Roosevelt's statement in a speech at Kingston Canada, that "the people of the United States will not stand idly by if domination of Canadian soil is threatened by any other empire." [35]

13. *Congressional Resolution of 1940 on transfers of territory in the Western Hemisphere*

The collapse of the Low Countries, France, and Denmark in 1940 aroused serious concern in the Americas. Seizure by Hitler of the American possessions of these countries, it was felt, would pose not only a grave threat to the Panama Canal and the Caribbean trade routes but also to the mainland of the United States. Congress promptly passed a resolution expressing opposition to the transfer of territory in the Western hemisphere from one non-American power to another. The

---

[33] *Id.*, pp. 30–31.
[34] Bailey, *op. cit. supra*, p. 684.
[35] *Id.*, 636.

resolution, which had been drafted by the Department of State with the President's approval, declared:[36]

"That the United States would not recognize any transfer, and would not acquiesce in any attempt to transfer, any geographic region of this hemisphere from one non-American power to another non-American power; and

"That if such transfer or attempt to transfer should appear likely, the United States shall, in addition to other measures, immediately consult with the other American republics to determine upon the steps which should be taken to safeguard their common interests."

14. The Greenland Action—1941

In April 1941, United States forces occupied the Danish possession of Greenland. This action was taken pursuant to an agreement signed by Secretary of State Hull, acting on behalf of the United States, and the Danish Minister in Washington.[37] The agreement noted the danger that Greenland might be converted into a base of aggression against American states and recognized the responsibility of the United States to assist in the maintenance of the existing status of Greenland. Article I of the Agreement provided:[38]

"The Government of the United States of America reiterates its recognition of and respect for the sovereignty of the Kingdom of Denmark over Greenland. Recognizing that as a result of the present European war there is danger that Greenland may be converted into a point of aggression against nations of the American Continent, the Government of the United States of America, having in mind its obligations under the Act of Habana signed on July 30, 1940, accepts the responsibility of assisting Greenland in the maintenance of its present status."

The Hitler-dominated government in Denmark disavowed the agreement as contrary to its constitution. Mr. Hull replied that the Denmark government was acting under duress and refused to acknowledge that the agreement was invalid.

15. Act of Havana of 1940; implementing treaty of 1942

After the defeat of France, representatives of the American states, convening in Havana in July 1940, adopted the Act of Havana, by which they agreed to prevent by collective action, or by unilateral action if necessary, changes in the control of territory in the Western Hemisphere as a result of the European hositilities. The Act was adopted in con-

[36] Logan, *An American Security Principle*, 327 (1961).

[37] Department of State Bulletin, vol. 4, No. 94, pp. 445–447 (April 12, 1941).

[38] Id., 445.

nection with the negotiation of a treaty thereafter ratified by fourteen states—the necessary two-thirds—in 1942.[39] It provided that if it appeared that American possessions of European powers might fall into the hands of an Axis power, they could be taken over and administered jointly by the American republics as trustees. In the event that the situation called for it, an individual state, such as the United States, could assume temporary control.

May 22, 1968

Professor Abram Chayes
Harvard Law School
Cambridge, Massachusetts

Dear Abe:

I read the other day in a bulletin from the American Society of International Law that you are doing a study of the background and development of the Cuban missile crisis. I happen to know a little of the story that you might not otherwise unearth, so I thought I would write you about it for whatever it may be worth.

President Kennedy signed my commission as Assistant Attorney General on August 6, 1962. My first job of any significance was given me by Bob Kennedy about mid-August. He told me there had been a lot of reports, as I knew, of missiles in Cuba, and while all the reports had proved to be about defensive, short-range missiles, it was thought that maybe the President ought to issue some sort of warning statement to the Soviet Union so that it would know in advance that we would not tolerate the installation of long-range ballistic missiles. Before doing that, he said, it was thought that we ought to do a serious study of whether the United States could, as a matter of international law, take action to prevent long-range missiles from being installed in Cuba, and perhaps of what form that action might take. . . . Sometime after the middle of August, I delivered to Bob a rather lengthy memo, together with a shorter memo attached to the front page and a draft of a Presidential statement.

In substance, the memorandum said that the United States could, under the principle of self-defense, take forcible action if necessary to prevent the installation of offensive weapons in the Western Hemisphere by the Soviet Union. In this connection, I emphasized that it would be of extreme importance to try to involve the OAS in whatever action was required; that the venture would be extremely difficult to defend legally if the U.S. acted unilaterally, but almost easy if action were taken by the

[39] Bemis *op. cit. supra* pp. 513–514 [Author's note: The reference is apparently to S. F. Bemis, A Short History of American Foreign Policy (1959)].

OAS. On the question of what action could be taken, I said the crux of the matter was the principle of proportionality. What was done would be sound legally if it was closely geared to the threat—if it was the least aggressive, least violent, narrowest response that would be adequate to meet the threat. To meet the problem posed by shipment of missiles, I suggested what I called a "vist-and-search blockade" which would assert the right to stop only traffic carrying offensive weapons. I believe the memo also said such a blockade should, if possible, be imposed at a time when suspected ships could turn back if they wished to avoid a confrontation, and that we should privately offer to make quiet inspections within the Soviet Union, through consular officials, to avoid abrasive contacts on the high seas so far as possible.

When I delivered the memo and other papers to Bob he engaged me in conversation about the problem and I told him I thought the best idea I had had was the "vist-and-search blockade" idea. This, I explained, would be unlike a blockade in the usual sense in that all normal commercial and even defensive military traffic could pass; we would assert the right to stop only traffic carrying missiles and other offensive weapons.

I believe the "vist-and-search blockade" idea was spelled out at least to some extent in both the long and the short memoranda. I am sure both are still in the files of the Office of Legal Counsel, and perhaps you could get them from Frank Wozencraft if they are of interest. Following Nick's practice, these memoranda were handled with the greatest possible care but were not formally classified, at least as I recall.

Bob proceeded to send copies of the longer memo and the proposed statement to various people in the government. I know the President and Rusk got copies, and I believe McNamara and Dillon were also on the list. In view of this distribution, I would guess Bundy and Allen Dulles were included.

On Labor Day, 1962, Nick and I met with Rusk at Bob's request to discuss the memo and the problem. I recall the day because we were all in sport shirts since it was a holiday. I recall discussing spot bombing and the partial blockade idea as well as the basic legal question.

Sometime in early September, there was a meeting in the Cabinet Room at the White House to discuss the proposed Presidential statement. The President was there, with Bundy; State was represented by Ed Martin, Justice by Bob, Nick and myself. Others present included Douglas Dillon and some people from the CIA. We discussed the statement and the President was critical of our draft because it mentioned the Monroe Doctrine. "The Monroe Doctrine," he snapped at me, "What the hell is that?" I mumbled some answer about its legal significance, but it was clear that whatever it was or meant, he didn't want to mention it in his statement.

After some discussion the President asked Bundy to work with a group of us and bring him a revised draft. Bundy, Nick, Dillon, Martin and I and a few others repaired to Bundy's basement office and Bundy dictated a draft while the rest of us made suggestions. I remember that Martin seemed testy and harassed, as if he resented having so many cooks in the meeting. We then went back upstairs, the President made some changes, and the statement was released almost immediately.

The statement was to the general effect that so far there was no evidence that the Soviet Union had sent anything to Cuba but defensive weaponry. "Were it to be otherwise," it went on, "the gravest questions would arise." Whether the final version specifically mentioned long-range missiles, I do not now recall.

When the actual crisis arose, I was in Oxford, Mississippi, where I had gone for the confrontation and riots of September 30 and October 1. I remained behind to work with Ramsey Clark on the clean-up, and ultimately returned to Washington on a flight leaving Memphis late Friday night, arriving about 5:00 A.M. Saturday. When we arrived, I called Justice to see whether there were any messages but there were none. By chance I remarked that I was sure there was no one in my office at that hour; the operator said, "Wait a minute, I'll ring," and lo and behold, Harold Reis answered.

I asked Harold what in the world he was doing there and he said he couldn't tell me over the telephone. Actually, the photographs of the missiles had arrived the previous Thursday, and Nick, Harold and Leon Ulman were working all night converting my old memo into one that would be more suitable for eventual public release and that would be geared to the facts that were then known.

I spent that Monday working with John MacNaughton at Defense on the Presidential Proclamation and various orders necessary to put what was then known as "quarantine" into effect. I believe it was John who told me that the President himself had thought of the name "quarantine" for what was to be done. That night, of course, the President went on national television and told the country what was happening.

As a result of the events I have recounted, I have at various times claimed to be the "inventor" of the device that came to be known as the quarantine. I saw in last week's *Life* that McNamara told an interviewer he and Gilpatric thought up the idea over lunch one day in mid-October. When the interviewer sought to pin him down on this, however, apparently he said something to the effect that you can never be sure who really thought of things like this; you forget who said what at various times and cannot really be sure where you got the idea. I thought as I read this passage that perhaps McNamara had had a glimmer of a recollection of having read or heard of my August memorandum.

So there you are. I hope it is of some use to you. It certainly has been fun to recall.

Sincerely,
Norbert A. Schlei

APPENDIX II

DRAFT MEMORANDUM OF THE LEGAL
ADVISER DATED 9/29/62
ON
LEGAL ISSUES INVOLVED IN OAS
SURVEILLANCE OVERFLIGHTS OF CUBA

The legal issues concerning OAS surveillance overflights of Cuba group themselves into three principal categories:

(1) The power of the Organ of Consultation under the Rio Treaty to authorize surveillance overflights;
(2) The bearing of the United Nations Charter;
(3) The potential effect on the United States legal position as to the Guantanamo base.

(1) *The Rio Treaty*

Under the Chicago Civil Aviation Convention and general international law, the air space over the territory of a state is subject to the sovereign power of the state. The state controls entry into its airspace. Intrusions without its consent are unlawful.

This general rule is, however, subject to any treaty arrangements to which a particular state may be a party. In the case of Cuba, these include the Inter-American Treaty of Reciprocal Assistance, the Rio Treaty. Article 6 of the Treaty reads as follows:

"If the inviolability or the integrity of the territory or the sovereignty or political independence of any American State should be affected by an aggression which is not an armed attack or by an extra-continental or intra-continental conflict, or by any other fact or situation that might endanger the peace of America, the Organ of Consultation shall meet immediately in order to agree on the measures which must be taken in case of aggression to assist the victim of the aggression or, in any case, the measures which should be taken for the common defense and for the maintenance of the peace and security of the Continent."

Action may be taken by the Organ of Consultation under this Article "by a vote of two-thirds of the Signatory States which have ratified the Treaty." (Article 17)

The language of Article 6 seems to distinguish between two types of situations: first, "aggression which is not armed attack,* "and, second, a conflict or "any other fact or situation that might endanger the peace of America." The present situation in Cuba probably can not be said to fall into the first category. It can, however, be subsumed under the heading of a "fact or situation that might endanger the peace of America." In fact, the resolutions at Caracas and Punte del Este may be said in combination to have made that determination.

Article 8 of the Treaty specifies the kinds of action that may be taken in Article 6 situations:

> "For the purposes of this Treaty, the measures on which the Organ of Consultation may agree will comprise one or more of the following: recall of chiefs of diplomatic missions; breaking of diplomatic relations; breaking of consular relations; partial or complete interruption of economic relations or of rail, sea, air, postal, telegraphic, telephonic, and radiotelephonic or radiotelegraphic communications; and use of armed force."

The list is subject to the qualification that "no State shall be required to use armed force without its consent." (Article 20)

The structure and history of the Rio Treaty are such as to indicate that this listing in Article 8 is an all-inclusive statement of the measures available to the Organ of Consultation in Article 6 situations. The United States has expressly maintained this position. The Report of the United States Rio Treaty Delegation records:

> ". . . The permissive character of the provision as originally drafted was changed to make it clear that the measures which may be agreed upon 'will comprise one or more of the following.'
>
> "Thus, in agreeing upon measures to be taken in a given situation under the treaty, the organ of consultation is, with one exception (contemplated in Article 7 in the event of an inter-American conflict), required to select from those enumerated in Article 8."

If surveillance overflights can fairly be brought within one of the classes, enumerated in Article 8, an overflight of Cuba pursuant to a resolution of the Organ of Consultation acting under Article 6 would not be unlawful intrusion into Cuban national airspace.

Three questions of special difficulty arise:

(a) *Can surveillance overflights be brought within any of the categories listed in Article 8?* It is clear that the only category which might be applicable is the last one—"use of armed force". A treaty which contemplates the use of force as the ultimate sanction should be taken to authorize lesser activities associated with military action. Surveillance and reconnaissance are such activities. Thus, surveillance overflights even though

* Article 3 deals with armed attack.

carried on by unarmed planes, are measures within the category of "use of armed force".

It should be noted however, that both in the OAS and in other international forums, the argument is likely to be pressed that surveillance overflight through national airspace is not a sanction available to the Organ of Consultation, since it is not specifically enumerated in Article 8.

(b) *Can Cuba raise any objection to action by the Organ of Consultation by reason of her suspension from participation in the organs of the OAS?* The action at Punta del Este did not expel Cuba from the Organization nor release her from obligations under existing treaties. The sole effect of the action was to preclude representatives of the present Government of Cuba from participating in the meetings of the various organs of the inter-American system. Cuba's international obligations remain intact.

On the other hand, Cuba and her defenders can argue that to the extent that the Rio Treaty contemplated sanctions against a member, that state would at least have the right to defend itself in a forum established by the Treaty. It would not be tried *in absentia*. More broadly, it may be urged that the OAS could not deprive Cuba of the benefits and privileges of the inter-American system and still hold her to the burdens and restrictions on the ordinary scope of sovereign rights. These arguments are likely to command considerable appeal. In response, it may be noted that Cuba has taken no formal action to denounce or abrogate the Rio Treaty or any other inter-American treaty or to withdraw from the OAS. Important rights and obligations running in her favor by virtue of the treaties, other than the right to sit in the organs of the inter-American system, still subsist.

(c) *Would Cuba have a basis for objecting to surveillance overflights if the action of the Organ of Consultation were only recommendatory in character?* As has been shown above, a resolution of the Organ of Consultation prescribing surveillance overflights may be regarded as recommendatory only, either because the present situation in Cuba does not amount to "aggression" within the meaning of Article 6, or because the overflight is a use of armed force to which, according to Article 20, no state can be compelled without its consent. However, even in that case, the position of Cuba would not be changed. The recommendatory character of a measure affects only the obligation of the states to participate in carrying it out, not the obligation of the state against which it is directed. This appears most clearly in connection with the Article 20 provision exempting a state from the obligation to use armed force without its consent. This voluntary aspect could hardly be thought to relieve the offending state from its obligation to accept the judgment of the Organ. Otherwise the actions of the Organ would be vitiated in the most serious cases, those calling for the use of armed force.

Thus, in the present case, the sole effect of holding the action of the

Organ to be recommendatory would be to relieve other American states of any obligation to participate in the surveillance overflights.

(2) *The United Nations Charter*

(a) *Threat or use of force*—The United Nations Charter provides that the obligations under it shall prevail over any conflicting international obligations. Similarly by its own terms, the Rio Treaty subordinates its provisions to those of the Charter. Analysis of the validity of surveillance overflights must, therefore, take into account the provisions of the Charter, in particular, Article 2(4) in which the Member States undertake to "refrain in their international relations from the threat or use of force against the territorial integrity or political independence of any State or in any other manner inconsistent with the purposes of the United Nations."

In my view, surveillance overflight, as such, does not involve the threat or use of force within the meaning of this Article. Neither the purpose nor the effect of such activity would be to bring hostile force to bear against the country under surveillance. Nor would it constitute a threat that force would be used unless that country bent to the will of the overflying powers. It would be a measure necessary for the common defense under Article 6 of the Rio Treaty. The sole purpose would be to gain information, information that would itself be used only for defensive military preparations. This position would gain in strength if the surveillance were accomplished by high-flying unarmed planes like the U-2, known to be without offensive capability.

There is a certain difficulty in maintaining that overflight activity is the use of armed force for the purposes of Article 8 of the Rio Treaty, but is not the threat or use of force within the meaning of Article 2(4) of the UN Charter. But this apparent inconsistency can be resolved in terms of the differing purposes of the two provisions.

(b) *Potential Cuban countermeasures*—We may anticipate that any intrusion into Cuban airspace will provoke countermeasures from the Cuban Government and her allies. If, as has been argued above, overflights carried out pursuant to an action of the Organ of Consultation under Article 6 of the Rio Treaty are lawful, it would appear that Cuba would not be justified in taking action to interfere with the flight. This conclusion, too, would be strongest in the case of a U-2 type overflight where the reconnaissance plane was obviously no offensive threat. In such a case, Cuba could not plausibly claim that an attempt to shoot down or divert the plane was action taken in defense against armed attack.

On the other hand, surveillance overflight might be carried out by less innocuous looking aircraft. RB-47's or other combat type aircraft flying at lower altitudes might reasonably seem, to Cuban military forces, to be engaged in an attack mission. If so, Cuba would have a strong case for regarding the overflight as a threat of force and for taking self-defensive action against it. The case would not be altered even if the OAS pilots in fact had no intention to attack and even if the fact that the mission was limited to reconnaissance had been announced in advance. In circumstances of such apparent danger, no nation could reasonably be required to rely on the good faith of others.

If the overflight itself was not wrongful, in logic it would seem that armed action to protect the planes against Cuban countermeasures would also be permissible. In fact, however, when these consequences— amounting in effect to full scale air war—are predictable, it becomes very difficult to defend the decision to launch the overflight in the first place as consistent with the Charter obligation to refrain from the use or threat of force.

Once countermeasures had been taken against an overflight, whether ground-to-air or air-to-air, nice analysis of the legality of counter-countermeasures would become increasingly academic. Neither side could be said to have surrendered its right to self-defense. The situation would lend itself to rapid escalation. The onus would inevitably be upon the party setting in motion a chain of events having these foreseeable consequences.

(c) *Security Council Jurisdiction*—Article 53 of the UN Charter provides:

> "The Security Council shall, where appropriate, utilize such regional arrangements or agencies for enforcement action under its authority. But no enforcement action shall be taken under regional arrangements or by regional agencies without the authorization of the Security Council . . ."

If surveillance overflights were to be considered "enforcement action", Security Council approval, obviously not obtainable, would be required.

There has never been any authoritative definition of "enforcement action" and the few precedents bearing on the question are unclear. In the two cases which have come before the Council—one involving sanctions against the Dominican Republic and the other the suspension of Cuba from OAS participation—the United States took the position that no enforcement action was involved. Although in neither case did the Security Council formally adopt this view of the matter, it acted in accordance with the United States position and declined to review the OAS action. Surveillance overflight is distinguishable in many ways from the sanctions heretofore considered by the Security Council. The surveillance flights are not designed to compel the government against which they are directed to take or desist from taking some action so as to comply with international obligations or with the authoritative order of an international body.

In reporting the Organ of Consultation action to the Security Council, in accordance with the terms of Article 5 of the Rio Treaty, the OAS would make clear that this action was not intended as enforcement action. Any proposal that the Security Council should, nevertheless, consider the matter as once coming under Article 53, would be subject to veto.

(3) *The United States Base at Guantanamo*

A subsidiary question arises as to the relation of surveillance overflights to the U.S. base rights at Guantanamo. In my view, if overflights were to be authorized by the Organ of Consultation, we should not employ Guantanamo as a base either for the planes engaged in surveillance themselves or for protection or support of those planes. It would be very difficult to maintain that under the Guantanamo Treaty the Cuban government granted the right to use the base against itself. Such use of the base would seriously weaken our legal position in defense of our base rights.

APPENDIX III

DEPARTMENT OF STATE MEMORANDUM: LEGAL BASIS FOR THE QUARANTINE OF CUBA*

The quarantine against shipments of offensive weapons to Cuba has been imposed by the United States in accordance with a recommendatory resolution of the Organ of Consultation established by the Inter-American Treaty of Reciprocal Assistance (Rio Treaty). The validity of the action in international law depends on affirmative answers to two questions:

(1) Was the action of the Organ of Consultation authorized by the Rio Treaty; and

(2) Is the action consistent with the provisions of the UN Charter to which the Rio Treaty is by its own terms and by the terms of the Charter subordinate?

1. *Authorization Under the Rio Treaty*

The Rio Treaty, together with related agreements, constitute the Inter-American system. The paramount purpose of this system, as stated in the Treaty, is:

> "to assure peace, through adequate means, to provide for effective reciprocal assistance to meet armed attacks against any American State, and . . . to deal with threats of aggression against any of them."

The Treaty provides for collective action, not only in the case of armed attack, which is covered by Article 3, but also:

> "If the inviolability or the integrity of the territory or the sovereignty or political independence of any American State should be affected by an aggression which is not an armed attack . . . or by any other fact or situation that might endanger the peace of America. . . ." (Article 6.)

In such cases, the Organ of Consultation, comprised of the Foreign Ministers of the Member States or representatives specifically designated for the purpose, is to,

> "meet immediately in order to agree on the measures which must be taken in case of aggression to assist the victim of the aggression or, in any case, the measures which should be taken for the common

* Prepared by Office of Legal Adviser, Dept. of State (Oct. 23, 1962).

defense and for the maintenance of the peace and security of the Continent." (Article 6.)

The Organ of Consultation acts "by a vote of two-thirds of the Signatory States which have ratified the Treaty." (Article 17.)

The Treaty is equally explicit as to the measures which may be taken by the Organ of Consultation in any case covered by Article 6. These measures are listed in Article 8 and specifically include "use of armed force". Article 20 further specifies that decisions to take any of the measures listed in Article 8 shall be binding except that "no State shall be required to use armed force without its consent."

The action of the OAS in the present case falls readily within the framework of the procedures established by the Treaty. The Inter-American system has long recognized that the adherence by the present Government of Cuba to Sino-Soviet Communism is inconsistent with the principles of the Inter-American system, and has created a situation endangering the peace of the hemisphere. As early as the Seventh Meeting of Foreign Ministers of the Organization of American States in 1960, the Organization "condemned the intervention or the threat of intervention of extra-continental communist powers in the hemisphere . . . ." The Eighth Meeting, at Punta del Este in 1962, went further. It declared that "the continental unity and democratic institutions of the hemisphere are now in danger." The source of that danger was the "subversive offensive of communist Governments." Among the "outstanding facts in this intensified offensive" was "the existence of a Marxist–Leninist government in Cuba which is publicly aligned with the doctrine and foreign policy of the communist powers." (Resolution I, Final Act, Eighth Meeting of Consultation of Ministers of Foreign Affairs Serving as Organ of Consultation in Application of the Inter-American Treaty of Reciprocal Assistance.)

At that meeting, the Organization took the first collective measures designed to deal with the threat. It prohibited all trade in arms with Cuba, and excluded the present government of that country from participation in the organs of the Inter-American system.

More recently, on October 2 and 3 of this year, the Foreign Ministers of the American States, meeting informally in Washington, reiterated that "the Soviet Union's intervention in Cuba threatens the unity of the Americas and its democratic institutions" and that this called "for the adoption of special measures, both individual and collective."

Against this background the Council of the Organization of American States met on October 23 and constituted itself as Organ of Consultation in accordance with Article 12 of the Rio Treaty. The Organ considered the evidence before it of the secret introduction of Soviet strategic missiles into Cuba in the face of Soviet and Cuban assurances to the contrary. It concluded that it was confronted with a situation that might endanger the peace of America within the meaning of Article 6. This considered judgment brought into play the authority to take one or more of the measures listed in Article 8. The resolution adopted by the Organ exercises this authority. It recommends

"that the member states, in accordance with Articles 6 and 8 of the Inter-American Treaty of Reciprocal Assistance, take all measures, individually and collectively including the use of armed force which they may deem necessary to ensure that the Government of Cuba cannot continue to receive from the Sino-Soviet powers military material and related supplies which may threaten the peace and security of the Continent and to prevent the missiles in Cuba with offensive capability from ever becoming an active threat to the peace and security of the Continent."

The recommendation contained in the Resolution for the use of armed force if necessary was thus fully authorized by the terms of the Rio Treaty and adopted in accordance with its procedures. The quarantine being imposed is specifically designed "to ensure that the Government of Cuba cannot continue to receive from the Sino-Soviet powers" the offensive weapons which threaten the peace and security of the Continent. It represents a minimal use of force to achieve the stated objectives. The United States action thus falls within the terms of the OAS Resolution.

2. The UN Charter

(a) Regional Organizations

The Resolution of the Organ of Consultation and the quarantine imposed by the United States pursuant to that Resolution are entirely consistent with the Charter of the United Nations.

The Charter specifically recognizes regional organizations and assigns to them an important place in carrying out the purposes of the United Nations. Article 52(1) states that

"Nothing in the present Charter precludes the existence of regional arrangements or agencies for dealing with such matters relating to the maintenance of international peace and security as are appropriate for regional action, provided that such arrangements or agencies and their activities are consistent with the Purposes and Principles of the United Nations."

Article 52(2) provides that United National Members that have entered into "such arrangements" or who have constituted "such agencies" must "make every effort to achieve pacific settlement of local disputes through such regional arrangements or by such regional agencies before referring them to the Security Council." Paragraph 3 of the same Article requires the Security Council to "encourage the development of pacific settlement of local disputes through such regional arrangements or by such regional agencies . . . ." Article 54 provides that, "The Security Council shall at all times be kept fully informed of activities undertaken or in contemplation under regional arrangements or by regional agencies for the maintenance of international peace and security." In accordance with this provision, the Organ of Consultation provided that the Security Council would be informed of the contents of the Resolution of October 23rd.

The Charter limits the activities of regional organizations only in the Article 52(1) proviso that such activities must be "consistent with the Purposes and Principles of the United Nations." The Rio Treaty plainly meets this requirement. It was enacted by the High Contracting Parties "to improve the procedure for the pacific settlement of their controversies," in full accord with Article 52(2). The High Contracting Parties expressly reiterated "their will to remain united in an inter-American system consistent with the purposes and principles of the United Nations." The Resolution and its implementation by the quarantine are in complete accordance with those purposes and principles. These measures are designed, in the opening words of the Charter, "to maintain international peace". They represent "effective collective measures for the prevention and removal of threats to the peace." Article 1(1).

The importance of regional agencies in the maintenance of peace and security was recognized in the earliest conceptions of the United Nations. The draft proposal which was prepared at the initial conference at Dumbarton Oaks is virtually the same as Chapter VIII of the Charter.

The framers of the Charter met in San Francisco in 1945 after the basic outlines of the most significant regional arrangement, the Organization of American States, were already established. The meeting was held subsequent to the Conference of the American Republics at which the Act of Chapultepec was approved. This Act recommended the execution of a treaty to establish a regional arrangement, and specifically provided that the "use of armed force to prevent or repel aggression" constituted "regional action which might appropriately be taken by the regional arrangements." The debates at the San Francisco Conference concerning regional organizations were held against this background, and the Organization of American States provided the principal context for the discussions.

When Article 52 was debated at the San Francisco Conference, the Chairman of the committee charged with considering regional arrangements, speaking as the delegate of Colombia, made the following statement concerning the relationship between the Inter-American system and Chapter VIII of the Charter:

"The Act of Chapultepec provides for the collective defense of the hemisphere and establishes that if an American nation is attacked all the rest consider themselves attacked. Consequently, such action as they may take to repel aggression, authorized by the article which was discussed in the subcommittee yesterday, is legitimate for all of them. Such action would be in accord with the Charter, by the approval of the article, and a regional arrangement may take action, provided it does not have improper purposes as, for example, joint aggression against another state. From this, it may be deduced that the approval of this article implies that the Act of Chapultepec is not in contravention of the Charter."

No delegate disputed this statement and it must be viewed as generally accepted. The very language of the Act of Chapultepec as well as its purposes were adopted by the Rio Treaty. It is evident that the Treaty created the very type of arrangement contemplated by the Charter.

The records of the Conference reveal that a major role was envisaged for regional arrangements under the Charter. Mr. Perez, the Minister of Foreign Affairs of Venezuela, said, "It is in the interests of all that any conflicts which may arise should be solved as quickly as possible in a satisfactory manner, and no one doubts that regional systems are most appropriate to this effect." The delegate from Mexico, Ambassador Najera noted, "In the chapter to which I am referring, the first consideration of the delegations of the American nations was to safeguard their greatest achievement, the most precious flower of cooperation for security through peaceful means." And the delegate of the United States, Senator Arthur Vandenburg, stated emphatically, "In my view we have infinitely strengthened the world organization by thus enlisting within its overall supervision, the dynamic resources of these regional affinities."

The history of events since the San Francisco Conference demonstrates the wisdom of the Charter's framers in entrusting to regional organizations the responsibility for handling regional disputes. Such organizations have close contact with the problems within their regions and thus can exercise considered and informed judgment in dealing with these problems. The Organization of American States is the prime example of this. The political process by which it must operate ensures that action will only be taken after careful analysis. Measures to protect peace and security can only be directed or recommended by a vote of two-thirds of the High Contracting Parties. Article 20 of the Treaty expressly provides that no State may be directed to use armed force without its consent. The Organ of Consultation may only recommend but cannot compel the use of armed force. By the presence of such safeguards, this regional organization is able to take effective action with assurance that such action will be consistent with the limitations imposed by the United Nations Charter. It has taken such action in regard to

Cuba by its October 23 Resolution, as implemented by the United States quarantine.

(b) *Article 53*

Article 53(1) of the UN Charter provides:

> "The Security Council shall, where appropriate, utilize such regional arrangements or agencies for enforcement action under its authority. But no enforcement action shall be taken under regional arrangements or by regional agencies without the authorization of the Security Council. . . ."

The quarantine measures here under consideration as approved by the Organ of Consultation do not constitute "enforcement action". Accordingly, these measures do not require Security Council authorization.

Twice before the Security Council has rejected the contention that the activities of a regional organization constituted "enforcement Action" within the meaning of Article 53 of the Charter. In September, 1960, the Council met to consider an allegation by the Soviet Union that a decision of the Organ of Consultation to take certain diplomatic and embargo measures against the Government of the Dominican Republic constituted "enforcement action". The Security Council did not accept that allegation. Earlier this year, Cuba asked the Security Council to consider decisions taken by the American Republics at Punta del Este, claiming that they required Security Council authorization. Again the Council disagreed.

Thus, it appears from the practice of the Security Council, that measures taken by a regional organization to deal with a threat to the peace, are not necessarily "enforcement action" even though they are obligatory in character. When, as here, they are recommendatory in character, it is clear that they cannot involve "enforcement action".

The construction of the phrase "enforcement action" is supported by its use elsewhere in the Charter. The expression appears at several places in the Charter in addition to Article 53. For example, Article 2, paragraph 5 obligates the Members of the United Nations to "refrain from giving assistance to any state against which the United Nations is taking preventive or enforcement action". And Article 5 provides that

> "A Member of the United Nations against which preventive or enforcement action has been taken by the Security Council may be suspended from the exercise of the rights and privileges of membership by the General Assembly upon the recommendation of the Security Council."

The "preventive" and "enforcement" action mentioned in these articles refers to action which the Council is authorized to take under Article 40, 41, and 42. Article 40 provides for taking of "preventive action" in the form of provisional measures. Such measures are orders of the Council with which Member States are bound to comply. Articles 41 and 42 empower the Council to enforce its decisions by calling upon United Nations Members to apply certain measures or by taking action directly through air, sea, or land forces which are at the disposal of the Security Council. Again, in acting under Articles 41 and 42, the Security Council does more than recommend to Members steps which they might take to meet a threat to peace and security. Rather it decides upon measures and issues orders of enforcement which Member States are obligated under the Charter to carry out.

Council actions under Articles 40, 41, and 42 are to be distinguished from recommendations made by the Council under Article 39 or by the General Assembly in the discharge of its responsibilities as set forth in Chapter IV of the Charter. In the exercise of its powers under Article 10 and 11, the General Assembly has on a number of occasions in the past recommended the use of armed force. The actions of the UN to repel aggression in Korea and to maintain order in the Congo are two such occasions. These actions were taken despite the contention made long ago that such measures constituted "action" which could only be taken by the Security Council. Since the Assembly's powers are only recommendatory in the field of peace and security, the exercise of these powers by the Assembly could not be considered either "preventive" or "enforcement" action.

This distinction between a Security Council measure which is obligatory and constitutes "action," on the one hand, and a measure which is recommended either by the Council or by the General Assembly on the other, is supported by the Advisory Opinion of the International Court of Justice, "Certain Expenses of the United Nations" (July 20, 1962). The Court held that the measures taken by the GA and the Security Council in Suez and the Congo were not enforcement action, in part, because they were only recommendatory as to participating States. Specifically, the Court stated:

"The word 'action' must mean such action as is solely within the province of the Security Council. It cannot refer to recommendations which the Security Council might make, as for instance under Article 38, because the General Assembly under Article 11 has a comparable power. The 'action' which is solely within the province of the Security Council is that which is indicated by the title of Chapter VII of the Charter, namely 'Action with respect to threats to the peace, breaches of the peace, and acts of aggression'. If the word 'action' in Article 11, paragraph 2, were interpreted to mean that the General Assembly could make recommendations only of a general character affecting peace and security in the abstract, and not in relation to specific cases, the paragraph would not have provided that the General Assembly may make recommendations on questions brought before it by States or by the Security Council. Accordingly, the last sentence of Article 11, paragraph 2, has no application where the necessary action is not enforcement action."

Thus, in the context of United Nations bodies, "enforcement action" does not include action by a United Nations body which is not obligatory on all the Members. As used in Article 53(1), "enforcement action" refers to action by a regional organization rather than to action by an organ of the United Nations, but the words must be given the same meaning in this context. It follows that "enforcement action", as the phrase appears in Article 53(1), does not comprehend action taken by a regional organization which is only recommendatory to the Members of the Organization.

As was pointed out above, the Resolution authorizing the quarantine was agreed upon pursuant to Article 6 of the Rio Treaty. As a recommendation of the "use of armed force", it was specifically authorized by Article 8 of that Treaty. And it is, by the express terms of Article 20, the one measure which, when agreed upon by the Organ of Consultation, Member States are not obligated to carry out. Since States signatories of the Rio Treaty are not obligated to carry out the Resolution recommending quarantine, it does not constitute "enforcement action" under Article 53(1), and is therefore not subject to Security Council authorization.

COMMENT

Louis Henkin

PROFESSOR CHAYES has given us a rare 'insider's' view of the workings of law in a major international incident of our times. Deftly, he analyses, compares, and correlates various reports of the intensive deliberations that preceded decision, tells what several participants said about the influence of law on their views, and offers his own conclusions as to how the law shaped particular positions and the eventual decision.

Perhaps better than any previous study, Professor Chayes's demonstrates the difficulties in investigating how law works in the foreign-policy process. The making of U.S. policy in the Cuban missile crisis has been described by several participants and by observers and reporters who had access to other participants, with greater authority and in greater detail than perhaps any other decision of our time. And yet, Professor Chayes shows, the influence of law cannot be proved, let alone measured. One would have to go behind what participants said and did not say, probe motives, intentions, expectations; and one would still not achieve a confident judgment as to how, and how much, law weighed with each participant. Then one would have to add, perhaps multiply, the uncertainties of a number of participants. And how to determine which one had how much influence on the recommendation made to the President? How much did that recommendation with its uncertain legal component weigh with him? Or how much did law itself weigh with him directly?

And yet, though beyond proof in a court of law, beyond measure by any instruments or means, Professor Chayes makes dramatically evident that law mattered. Principally, of course, law restrained governmental action, at least directing choice among alternatives; he shows how law served as an obstacle to detour policy-makers from blatant violations, compelling them to circumvent or compromise. Each participant, of course, had his own measure as to how much of an obstacle law was to his desired policy and how close to violation he was willing to go, and his own estimate as to how close others, particularly the President, would be willing to go. Some of the President's advisers acquiesced in the quarantine because if it failed bombing would still be possible and effective. If so, with them at least, law restrained less; it did not reject one decision in favour of another, but only ordered priority between them. But Professor Chayes speculates that the United States would not in fact have bombed even if the quarantine had failed.

Professor Chayes also helps to destroy some misconceived distinctions between law and politics. All law, of course, is political: nations make law (rather than leave a matter unregulated) from a political judgment that it will be in their respective or common interests. How existing law would be interpreted, whether it should be violated, what kind or degree of violation should be perpetrated, are also political decisions subject to the constraints of law and the costs of violation in international society.

Not only the lawyer, but the student of politics and political processes, will be instructed especially by Professor Chayes's discussion of the legal case for the United States action in the missile crisis. His insights into the uses of justification should help dispel the cynicism which sees in it only instincts of hypocrisy. The need to justify, surely, helps keep governments from actions that cannot be justified; sometimes alternative justifications are available, implying different claims and commitments as to what the law is or ought to be, and the choice between them might also shape the action to be taken. The justification chosen here—the claim of the U.S., supported by the O.A.S., that the organization had a rightful say in the matter—also served as a significant communication: the Soviet Union was being told that the United States would insist on the removal of the missiles, that it thought it had legitimate case for its insistence, that it was not alone in that view.

Professor Chayes's story shows, too, how the choice of law in justification is sometimes determined by the comparative elasticity of the alternatives. I have seen no merit, and great danger, in the notion that Article 51 permits anticipatory self-defence; surely, any such exception would have to be limited to instances where there is ground to conclude, beyond reasonable doubt, that an armed attack is imminent, and the Cuban crisis could not be brought within any such exception without having it swallow whole the rule of Article 2(4). Since Article 51 was not sufficiently elastic, the Acting Legal Adviser turned to Chapter VIII, and proposed action accordingly. Whether the United States went to the O.A.S. to legitimize its proposed quarantine, or whether the O.A.S. was indicated for reasons of hemispheric policy, makes little difference. Recourse to the O.A.S. proved more malleable in law as well as more acceptable politics.

Whether the applicable law of regional organization was as malleable as the Acting Legal Adviser implied is a different question. The Cuban case was hard and special in several respects, producing less than good and general law. Soviet missiles in Cuba were an issue between the U.S. and Soviet Russia, with Cuba only the locus and focus of the dispute; Russia and the other countries whose vessels were heading for Cuba were not members of the O.A.S. or otherwise within the region, were not subject to the authority of the organization, and this dispute was probably not within the spirit and contemplation of Chapter VIII. The authority of the O.A.S., then, was far different here from what it was in the Dominican case later.

The claimed elasticity of the law of regional organizations also raises more fundamental questions. One path to justification admits that the U.S.–O.A.S. action was 'enforcement action' under Article 53 but enjoyed the required authorization of the Security Council since the Council failed to disown it. It is reasonable enough to suggest that the Charter is satisfied if the regional action is subsequently ratified by the Security Council, though that might encourage regional organizations not to seek authorization in advance, and even to act where subsequent ratification by the Council is hardly certain. (If Security Council approval did not in fact ensue, the regional enforcement action might be impossible to undo.) But, accepting subsequent ratification as authorization, it is hardly a short further step, as has been suggested, to find authorization by the Council where the Council would have approved but for the veto of a permanent member. That is quite a long step attempting to eliminate the veto in what is surely an important substantive matter. It is also not a short step to find authorization by the Security Council in 'failure to disapprove' where a majority vote to disapprove failed as the result of a veto: that a single negative vote by a Big Power should in effect serve as Security Council ratification of a regional enforcement action would stand Chapter VIII on its head.

A different justification had it that Security Council authorization was not necessary because, while the quarantine might have been enforcement action had it been commanded, the O.A.S. merely recommended it. But, if the United States could not lawfully impose the quarantine on its own authority, would a recommendation by the O.A.S. supply authorization to do so? There have been suggestions that just as the General Assembly asserted authority to act when the Security Council failed, regional organizations have similar authority as a result of the Council's failure. Even as regards the General Assembly, it is far from clear that its recommendation can supply authority to do what would be forbidden to individual members on their own; regional organizations have even less claim to legitimize force forbidden to its members by the U.N. Charter. The requirement in Article 53 of Security Council approval for 'enforcement action' underscores the import of Article 52(3) which apparently contemplates regional action only for the 'pacific settlement of local disputes'.

In principle, I would suggest, the authority of regional organizations must be sought not in legacy from the Security Council but more nearly in the sum of the powers of its members. Of course, combining the rights of its members under Article 51, a regional organization can mobilize them in collective self-defence against armed attack upon one of its members (or any other state), whether by another member or from the outside. By its charter, acquiesced in by all members and sanctioned by the U.N. Charter, a regional organization has authority and responsbility also to engage in peacekeeping and peaceful peacemaking. (While such activity is surely not forbidden to individual members either, regional action cannot be rebuffed and resisted as intervention, meddling.) The organization can perhaps press recalcitrant members that deviate from friendly relations, or even outside states that roil regional friendly relations, by means short of force. But, unless authorized by the U.N. Security Council, neither a directive nor a recommendation by a regional organization can legitimize force which is forbidden to its individual members by the Charter.

The limits I suggest, imposed by the language and history of the Charter, are indispensable where superpowers dominate. It is not that Article 53 is 'unworkable' when a Big Power is heavily involved; it is rather that the very existence of Big Powers threatens to distort the concept of regional organization, and the mantle designed for collective bodies exercising collective judgment will be claimed by 'solar systems'. The O.A.S., many believe, is a bona fide regional organization, not a rubber stamp for the United States. But, many believe, the same is not true of the Warsaw Pact in relation to the Soviet Union, yet on what basis, legal or political, would one deny its claim to be a regional organization? If an O.A.S. recommendation of a quarantine legitimizes it, why not a Warsaw Pact recommendation of action against Czechoslovakia? Suggestions that the legitimacy of a regional organization depends on degrees of independence or of integration within it are politically as well as legally hopeless. To allow the authority of a 'regional organization', effectively, to a major power able to dictate to its satellites will distort the U.N. Charter to whatever extent regional organizations are permitted to do what the dominant major power itself could not properly do. The safeguard, I believe, lies in limiting all regional organizations to peaceful peacemaking and peacekeeping, in denying to all regional organizations authority to use, direct, or recommend force where its individual members could not use such force, unless it is in fact authorized by the U.N. Security Council.

In the Cuban crisis, then, the O.A.S. action could not confer authority which the United States did not have. It represented principally political support, including, by implication, a collective judgment that the quarantine was lawful. That law too is not without ambiguity and malleability. Behind Cuba, as elsewhere, was the uncertainty of the scope of permissible uses of force when there is no armed attack justifying self-defence under Article 51. A strong case can indeed be made that no other unilateral uses of force are permitted. But the Charter forbids the use or threat of force 'against the territorial integrity or political independence of any state, or in any other manner inconsistent with the purposes of the United Nations'; not enough attention has been paid to these qualifying phrases. The quarantine was surely a threat if not a use of force; but was it against the political independence or territorial integrity of Cuba? Of Russia? Of other states shipping to Cuba? Or, alternatively, was it 'in any other manner inconsistent with the purposes of the United

Nations?' In other, more common contexts, is it a 'use of force' within the meaning of Article 2(4), and is it a use of force against the political independence or territorial integrity of the 'victim' state, to send airplanes to take hostages out of the Congo, or even Marines to safeguard lives when order has broken down in the Dominican Republic (assuming that to be what happened in 1965)? The question is not merely one of legitimate interpretation of the words in the light of their history; the important question is what limitation on such uses of force, assuming bona fide humanitarian (or other 'peaceful') purposes, are consistent with the spirit of the Charter and realistically viable in contemporary society?

Some may find grounds to differ with Professor Chayes in what he distils for emphasis and conclusion. It is indeed important that someone call the lawyers in; it is better indeed when they are in without being called, when their participation in the process of decision is routine and unfailing. To a large extent, however, the law is in even when the lawyers are not. The law is often subsumed or disguised in political or moral considerations that move policy-makers, considerations like those which helped make the law in the first instance. Experienced policy-makers, moreover, more or less knowingly assimilate what the law requires, in the gross at least, and it inevitably shapes their inclinations and deliberations.

Some will find that Professor Chayes has emphasized institutions at the expense of norms. Institutions too must heed norms. The analogy to constitutional law in not inapt, but there is more 'law' in constitutional law than some like to believe, though political institutions feel freer than judicial bodies to apply that law *ad hoc* without scrupulous regard to 'neutral principles'. The depreciation of norms also reflects a wider fallacy, a common misperception that sees only the uncertainty in international law, only the disorder in international society. International law is not always indeterminate. If it is 'more or less' at the peripheries, there is indeed a large centre of 'yes or no' which governs the conduct of governments, inspires few reasonable doubts, raises few serious issues.

Generalizations about international law drawn from the Cuban crisis must consider that the law there relevant—principally the law of the U.N. Charter forbidding the use or threat of force—is unique and radical law. It seeks to curb that international action which is most dramatic, most disorderly, and most costly, and which is taken as a last resort and for the highest stakes. It is law which was long in coming, and which many thought—and many think—is not viable and perhaps not desirable. But even—perhaps especially—that law is not all that indeterminate. Surely it was intended that Article 2(4) be a substantial substantive norm, that it should not merely order deliberations in the light of self-judging perceptions of 'necessity and proportion', but that it should guide conduct within narrow limits. The Cuban crisis may have uncovered uncertainties in the norm and challenged its applicability in dramatically exceptional contexts, but Cuba affirms rather than dilutes the norm as regards the clear cases to which it speaks. Before and since Cuba, despite continuing violence in internal wars and external interventions in such wars, states have in fact largely been governed by that norm, and the threshold of national interest that would lead to violation is higher than ever. Nothin in the Cuban crisis, or in the other events and transformations since 1945, suggests that the norm generally should be scrapped or diluted.

INDEX